Getting Approved for an SBA Commercial Mortgage Loan

Step-by-Step Strategies to Meet SBA Mortgage Requirements and Secure Funding

By Joseph G. Correa

Licensed Mortgage Broker, Finibi Mortgage

Copyright & Legal Notice

Published by Live Stronger Faster

The information provided in this book is for educational and informational purposes only and does not constitute financial, legal, tax, or investment advice. Although the author is a licensed mortgage professional, the content presented is general in nature and is not intended as personalized guidance for any specific individual, business, or financial situation.

The strategies, loan structures, and examples discussed in this book are illustrative and educational in nature. They are intended to demonstrate concepts related to SBA commercial mortgage financing, including SBA 7(a) and 504 loan programs, borrower qualification, debt service coverage analysis, property acquisition, refinancing, construction financing, and advanced loan structuring. These examples do not represent guaranteed approvals, loan terms, or outcomes. Results may vary significantly based on individual financial profiles, credit history, business performance, property type, market conditions, and lender-specific guidelines.

SBA loan programs are subject to eligibility requirements, regulatory guidelines, and changes established by the U.S. Small Business Administration and participating lenders. Borrowers are encouraged to consult directly with qualified financial, legal, and tax professionals before making any financing or investment decisions.

The author and publisher make no representations or warranties regarding the accuracy, completeness, or applicability of the content and disclaim any liability for errors, omissions, or outcomes resulting from the use or misuse of the information contained in this book.

First Edition, 2026

Table of Contents

Introduction

Securing approval for an SBA commercial mortgage loan is one of the most powerful financial moves a business owner or real estate investor can make, yet it is also one of the most misunderstood and intimidating processes in commercial finance. Many borrowers assume that SBA loans are difficult, slow, or nearly impossible to qualify for, when in reality, the process is highly structured, predictable, and strategic for those who understand how lenders evaluate risk and how to position themselves correctly. The difference between a denied application and a fully approved SBA commercial mortgage loan often has little to do with the borrower's income or credit alone and far more to do with preparation, presentation, and strategy. This book is designed to bridge that gap, giving you a clear, step-by-step roadmap to move from uncertainty to approval with confidence.

At its core, the SBA commercial mortgage approval process is about risk mitigation from the lender's perspective. Unlike conventional commercial loans, SBA loans are partially guaranteed by the government, which allows lenders to take on borrowers who may not meet traditional bank standards. However, this does not mean that the process is relaxed or lenient. In fact, SBA lenders follow strict underwriting guidelines that evaluate multiple layers of risk, including borrower strength, business performance, property viability, and global cash flow. Understanding how these factors interact is critical. Approval is not based on one single factor but rather the complete story your application tells. This book will teach you how to control that narrative.

One of the biggest mistakes borrowers make when applying for an SBA commercial mortgage loan is approaching the process reactively instead of proactively. Many applicants submit documents as requested, answer questions as they arise, and hope the lender will piece everything together favorably. This passive approach often leads to delays, confusion, and ultimately denial. Successful borrowers, on the other hand, take control of the process from the beginning. They understand what lenders are looking for before the application is even submitted, and they structure their financial profile, documentation, and deal in a way that aligns with SBA guidelines. This book will show you how to think like an underwriter, so you can prepare your file in advance and eliminate unnecessary obstacles.

Approval begins long before you fill out a loan application. It starts with understanding your borrower profile and identifying strengths and weaknesses. Your personal credit history, business financials, liquidity, industry experience, and management capability all play a role in how your application is perceived. Lenders want to see not only that you can repay the loan but also that you have the stability and expertise to operate the business or property successfully. Even if your profile is not perfect, there are proven strategies to strengthen your position. From improving credit scores and organizing financial statements to demonstrating compensating factors such as reserves or strong cash flow, small adjustments can significantly increase your chances of approval.

Another critical component of the SBA loan approval process is the business itself. Whether you are acquiring an existing business, refinancing commercial real estate, or purchasing an owner-occupied property, lenders will evaluate the income-producing ability of the business or property in detail. This includes analyzing historical financial statements, tax returns, and projected income. They want to ensure that the business generates enough cash flow to cover the loan payments with a comfortable margin. This concept, known as debt service coverage, is one of the most important metrics in SBA underwriting. In this book, you will learn how lenders calculate this ratio, what thresholds they look for, and how to structure your deal to meet or exceed those requirements.

Equally important is the structure of the deal itself. SBA loans are not one-size-fits-all, and the way a loan is structured can have a major impact on approval. This includes the loan amount, down payment, use of funds, collateral, and repayment terms. For example, a well-structured SBA 7(a) loan may allow for flexibility in use of proceeds, while an SBA 504 loan may offer long-term fixed rates for real estate purchases. Understanding which program to use and how to align it with your specific goals is essential. More importantly, knowing how to present your deal in a way that reduces perceived risk can make the difference between approval and denial. This book will guide you through these decisions with clarity and precision.

Documentation is another area where many borrowers struggle, yet it is one of the most controllable aspects of the approval process. SBA lenders require a comprehensive set of documents, including personal and business tax returns, financial statements, business plans, lease agreements, and more. Missing, incomplete, or inconsistent documentation can delay the process or raise red flags. However, when documents are organized, accurate, and aligned with the story you are presenting, they can significantly strengthen your application. This book will provide you with a clear checklist of required documents and best practices for preparing them in a way that meets lender expectations. In addition to financials and documentation, lenders place a strong emphasis on the borrower's experience and management capability. They want to know that you understand the business you are operating or acquiring. This is especially important for first-time business owners or investors entering a new industry. Demonstrating relevant experience, whether through prior work history, partnerships, or professional advisors, can help mitigate risk and improve your chances of approval. Even if you lack direct experience, there are strategic ways to position your background and build a support team that strengthens your application. This book will show you how to do that effectively.

Another often overlooked aspect of SBA loan approval is the importance of lender selection. Not all SBA lenders are the same. Some specialize in certain industries, loan sizes, or types of transactions. Others may have more flexible underwriting approaches or faster processing times. Choosing the right lender can significantly impact your experience and outcome. In this book, you will learn how to identify and approach lenders that are best suited to your specific deal, increasing your chances of approval while reducing friction in the process.

Timing also plays a critical role in the approval process. From initial application to final closing, SBA loans can take several weeks or even months to complete. Understanding the timeline and knowing what to expect at each stage can help you stay prepared and avoid unnecessary delays. More importantly, knowing how to anticipate lender requests and respond quickly can keep your file moving forward. This book will walk you through the entire approval timeline, from prequalification and underwriting to commitment and closing, so you can navigate each step with confidence.

Throughout this book, you will also gain insight into common pitfalls that lead to denials and how to avoid them. These include issues such as insufficient cash flow, poor credit history, lack of documentation, unrealistic projections, and misaligned deal structures. By understanding these risks in advance, you can take proactive steps to address them before they become obstacles. In many cases, a denied application is not the end of the road but rather an opportunity to restructure and resubmit with a stronger position. This book will teach you how to turn potential weaknesses into strengths.

Ultimately, getting approved for an SBA commercial mortgage loan is not about luck or guesswork. It is a strategic process that can be learned, mastered, and repeated. Once you understand how lenders think and what they require, you gain a significant advantage. You are no longer reacting to the process—you are controlling it. This shift in mindset is what separates successful borrowers from those who struggle. It allows you to approach each deal with clarity, confidence, and a higher probability of success. As you move through this book, you will begin to see the SBA approval process not as a barrier but as a system—a system designed to identify strong borrowers and viable deals. Your goal is to position yourself within that system in the most favorable way possible. By applying the strategies outlined in this book, you will be able to present a complete, compelling, and well-structured loan package that aligns with SBA guidelines and lender expectations.

This is where your journey toward approval truly begins. Whether you are purchasing your first owner-occupied property, acquiring a business, or expanding your commercial real estate portfolio, the principles in this book will serve as your foundation. The knowledge you gain here will not only help you secure your first SBA loan but will also empower you to repeat the process and scale your investments over time.

Approval is not reserved for a select few. It is available to those who are prepared, strategic, and informed. This book will show you exactly how to become that borrower.

Chapter 1

Understanding the SBA Approval Framework and How Lenders Think

The SBA commercial mortgage loan approval process is not random, subjective, or based on guesswork. It follows a structured framework that lenders use to evaluate every borrower and every deal with consistency and precision. To get approved, you must first understand how lenders think, what they prioritize, and how they measure risk. Once you understand this framework, you gain the ability to position yourself strategically rather than simply hoping your application meets the requirements. This chapter will walk you through the core pillars of SBA underwriting so you can begin thinking like a lender and preparing like a professional.

At the foundation of every SBA loan decision is risk assessment. Lenders are not just asking whether you want the loan or whether the deal looks good on the surface. They are asking a much more important question: what is the probability that this loan will be repaid in full and on time? To answer that question, they evaluate multiple layers of risk simultaneously. These layers include borrower strength, business performance, property stability, and overall deal structure. Each of these components contributes to the final decision, and weakness in one area can sometimes be offset by strength in another if properly presented.

The first major pillar lenders evaluate is the borrower profile. This includes your personal credit, financial history, liquidity, and overall financial behavior. Your credit score is often the first filter in the process, but it is not the only factor. Lenders are looking deeper into your credit report to understand patterns such as late payments, collections, or high utilization. A borrower with a 700 score and strong payment history may be viewed more favorably than someone with a higher score but inconsistent behavior. Beyond credit, lenders evaluate your liquidity, meaning how much cash or liquid assets you have available after closing. This serves as a safety net and demonstrates your ability to handle unexpected expenses.

The second pillar is business performance, which is especially critical when the loan involves an operating business. Lenders want to see stable and predictable income. They analyze tax returns, profit and loss statements, and balance sheets to determine whether the business generates enough income to support the proposed loan payment. Consistency is key. A business that shows steady or increasing revenue over time is far more attractive than one with volatile or declining performance. Even if the numbers are strong, lenders will also assess the sustainability of that income. They want to understand the business model, customer base, and industry trends to ensure the income will continue.

One of the most important metrics lenders use to evaluate business performance is the debt service coverage ratio, commonly referred to as DSCR. This ratio measures how much income is available to cover the loan payments. A DSCR of 1.25, for example, means that the business generates 25 percent more income than is required to pay the debt. This provides a cushion for the lender. If the ratio is too low, the loan becomes riskier. Understanding how this ratio is calculated and how to improve it is essential for approval, and it is something you will learn to master throughout this book.

The third pillar is the property or collateral. In SBA commercial mortgage loans, the property often serves as both an income-producing asset and collateral for the loan. Lenders evaluate the value of the property through an appraisal, but they also look at its usability, condition, and marketability. For owner-occupied properties, they want to ensure the space supports the business operations effectively. For investment-related components, they assess whether the property can maintain its value and generate income if needed. A well-located, functional property in a stable market significantly reduces risk from the lender's perspective. The fourth pillar is the deal structure. This includes how the loan is set up, including the loan amount, down payment, repayment terms, and use of funds. SBA loans are unique in that they allow for flexible structures, but that flexibility must still align with guidelines. A properly structured deal reduces risk and improves approval odds. For example, a higher down payment lowers the lender's exposure and shows borrower commitment. Similarly, clear and logical use of funds helps lenders understand exactly how the loan will benefit the business or property. When the structure makes sense, approval becomes much easier.

Another key concept in the SBA approval framework is global cash flow analysis. This goes beyond the business itself and looks at your entire financial picture, including personal income, other businesses, and existing debts. Lenders want to ensure that you can support the loan not only through the business but also through your overall financial situation if needed. This comprehensive approach provides a more accurate picture of risk and is one of the reasons SBA loans are both flexible and thorough.

Experience and management capability are also critical components of the approval process. Lenders are not just investing in a property or a set of financial statements—they are investing in you. They want to know that you have the knowledge, skills, and support system to operate successfully.

This is especially important for business acquisitions or new ventures. Demonstrating relevant experience, even indirectly, can significantly strengthen your application. If experience is limited, having a strong team of advisors or partners can help fill that gap.

Equally important is the story behind the numbers. Every SBA loan application tells a story, and lenders are trying to determine whether that story makes sense. Do the financials align with the business model? Does the projected growth match historical performance? Are there any inconsistencies that raise concerns? A well-prepared application presents a clear and consistent narrative that supports the numbers. This includes a strong business plan that explains how the loan will be used, how the business will grow, and how the loan will be repaid.

Documentation plays a vital role in supporting this story. Lenders rely on documentation to verify every aspect of your application. Missing or inconsistent documents can create doubt and slow down the process. On the other hand, a complete and well-organized file builds confidence and accelerates approval. This includes everything from tax returns and financial statements to legal documents and lease agreements. Attention to detail in this area can make a significant difference. Understanding the SBA approval framework is not just about meeting requirements—it is about exceeding expectations. When you know what lenders are looking for, you can go beyond simply qualifying and position yourself as a strong, low-risk borrower. This shift in approach changes everything. Instead of reacting to lender requests, you anticipate them. Instead of hoping for approval, you build a case for it.

As you move forward, remember that every deal is unique, but the principles remain the same. Borrower strength, business performance, property stability, and deal structure will always be at the core of the decision. By mastering these elements, you gain control over the outcome. You begin to see opportunities where others see obstacles, and you develop the ability to navigate the process with confidence.

This chapter sets the foundation for everything that follows. In the chapters ahead, you will dive deeper into each component of the approval process, learning specific strategies to strengthen your profile, structure your deals, and present your application effectively. The goal is not just to get approved once, but to develop a repeatable system that allows you to secure funding again and again as you grow your business and real estate portfolio.

Real-Life Math Example: SBA Loan Approval Scenario and Financial Breakdown

Imagine a borrower named David who owns a small but growing manufacturing business. David is looking to purchase a commercial property for $1,200,000 to house his operations and reduce long-term leasing costs. He decides to pursue an SBA 7(a) commercial mortgage loan to finance the purchase. The lender requires a 10 percent down payment, meaning David must contribute $120,000 of his own funds. The remaining $1,080,000 will be financed through the SBA loan.

David's business generates annual gross revenue of $900,000. After expenses, his net operating income is $180,000 per year. The proposed loan has an interest rate of 7.5 percent with a 25-year amortization. Based on these terms, the annual debt service, which includes principal and interest payments, is approximately $95,000. This is a critical number because it will be used to calculate the debt service coverage ratio.

To determine whether David qualifies, the lender calculates the DSCR by dividing the net operating income by the annual debt service. In this case, $180,000 divided by $95,000 results in a DSCR of approximately 1.89. This means David's business generates 89 percent more income than required to cover the loan payments, which is well above the typical minimum requirement of 1.25. From a cash flow perspective, this is a strong deal.

However, the lender does not stop there. They also evaluate David's personal financial situation. David has a credit score of 720, which is considered strong. He has $200,000 in savings before the down payment. After contributing $120,000, he will still have $80,000 in reserves. This is important because lenders want to see that borrowers have enough liquidity to cover several months of expenses in case of unexpected challenges.

Next, the lender reviews David's global cash flow. In addition to his business income, David has a small side investment property that generates $12,000 per year in net income. He also has personal expenses and existing debt obligations totaling $40,000 annually. When combining all sources of income and subtracting all obligations, David still shows a positive global cash flow, further strengthening his application.

The lender also evaluates the property itself. An appraisal confirms that the property is worth $1,200,000, matching the purchase price. The property is in a stable industrial area with strong demand, and it is well-suited for David's business operations. This reduces risk from a collateral perspective.

Now consider a scenario where David's numbers were slightly different. If his net operating income were only $120,000 instead of $180,000, the DSCR would drop to approximately 1.26. While this still meets the minimum requirement, it leaves very little margin for error. In this case, the lender may look for compensating factors such as higher reserves, a larger down payment, or additional income sources to justify approval.

If David wanted to improve his position, he could take several steps. He could increase his down payment to reduce the loan amount and lower the annual debt service. For example, if he increased his down payment to $200,000, the loan amount would drop to $1,000,000, reducing the annual payment and increasing the DSCR. Alternatively, he could work on increasing business profitability by reducing expenses or increasing revenue, which would directly improve the ratio.

This example demonstrates how all the components of SBA underwriting work together. It is not just about income or credit or the property alone. It is about how each piece fits into the overall picture. A strong DSCR, solid credit, adequate reserves, and a well-located property all contribute to a successful application.

By understanding these calculations and how lenders interpret them, you gain the ability to shape your deal before it is ever submitted. You can adjust variables, strengthen weak areas, and present a complete and compelling case for approval. This is the key to mastering the SBA loan process and achieving consistent success.

Chapter 2

Building a Strong Borrower Profile That Gets Approved

The foundation of every successful SBA commercial mortgage loan approval begins with the borrower. Before lenders analyze the business, the property, or even the structure of the deal, they evaluate the individual behind the application. This is because the borrower represents the ultimate source of responsibility for the loan. No matter how strong a deal appears on paper, lenders want to know that the person managing it has the financial discipline, experience, and reliability to execute successfully. In this chapter, you will learn how to build, strengthen, and position your borrower profile so that it aligns with SBA expectations and significantly increases your chances of approval.

Your borrower profile is composed of several key components: personal credit, liquidity, financial behavior, experience, and overall financial stability. Each of these elements contributes to how lenders perceive risk. The goal is not to be perfect in every category but to demonstrate consistency, responsibility, and the ability to manage financial obligations over time. Even borrowers with imperfections can be approved when their overall profile is structured correctly and supported by strong compensating factors.

Personal credit is often the first and most visible component of your borrower profile. While SBA loans are more flexible than conventional loans, lenders still use credit as an indicator of how you manage debt. A strong credit profile typically includes a history of on-time payments, low credit utilization, and a mix of credit accounts. However, lenders look beyond the score itself. They analyze patterns within your credit report. For example, a borrower with a few isolated late payments years ago may still be considered strong if recent behavior is consistent and positive. On the other hand, frequent recent delinquencies can raise red flags even if the score appears acceptable.

If your credit is not where it needs to be, there are strategic ways to improve it before applying. Paying down revolving balances, resolving collections, and ensuring all accounts are current can have a significant impact. Timing is also important. Even a 30- to 60-day improvement period can make a meaningful difference in how your application is viewed. The key is to approach credit improvement intentionally rather than assuming it cannot be changed.

Liquidity is another critical factor in your borrower profile. Lenders want to see that you have sufficient cash or liquid assets available both for the required down payment and for reserves after closing. This demonstrates financial stability and the ability to handle unexpected expenses. Reserves are especially important in SBA loans because they provide a cushion in case the business experiences temporary challenges. A borrower who closes with no remaining cash is considered high risk, even if other aspects of the application are strong.

Your financial behavior also plays a significant role. Lenders review bank statements to understand how you manage money on a day-to-day basis. They look for consistent deposits, controlled spending, and the absence of unexplained large withdrawals or overdrafts. This behavior tells a story about your financial discipline. Even if your income is strong, poor financial management can create concerns. On the other hand, steady and predictable activity builds confidence.

Experience is another key component that lenders evaluate closely. They want to know whether you have the knowledge and skills to operate the business or manage the property successfully. Direct experience in the same industry is ideal, but it is not always required. Transferable skills, such as management experience, financial oversight, or operational leadership, can also be valuable. If you lack direct experience, you can strengthen your profile by building a team that includes experienced partners, advisors, or key employees who can support the operation. Another important aspect of your borrower profile is your overall financial stability. This includes your income sources, existing debts, and long-term financial trends. Lenders look for consistency over time. A borrower who has demonstrated steady income and responsible financial management over several years is viewed as lower risk than someone with recent or unpredictable changes. Stability builds trust, and trust plays a significant role in the approval process.

One of the most powerful strategies for strengthening your borrower profile is identifying and highlighting compensating factors. These are strengths that can offset weaknesses in other areas. For example, if your credit score is slightly below ideal, strong liquidity or a high DSCR can help balance that risk. If your experience is limited, a strong management team or a well-performing business can compensate. The key is to present a complete picture that shows the lender why the overall risk is acceptable.

It is also important to understand the concept of personal guarantees in SBA lending. Most SBA loans require the borrower to personally guarantee the loan, which means you are personally responsible for repayment if the business cannot meet its obligations. This reinforces the importance of your borrower profile. Lenders are not just evaluating a business transaction—they are evaluating your personal commitment and accountability. Another factor that can influence your borrower profile is your history with lenders and financial institutions. A borrower who has successfully managed previous loans or maintained strong relationships with banks may have an advantage. This track record demonstrates reliability and can make lenders more comfortable extending credit. Even if you are new to SBA loans, building strong financial relationships over time can benefit you in the long run.

Preparation is key when building your borrower profile. This includes organizing your financial documents, reviewing your credit report, and addressing any potential issues before applying. It also involves understanding how lenders will view your profile and taking proactive steps to strengthen it. Waiting until the application process begins can limit your ability to make meaningful improvements.

Another important consideration is how you present your profile. This goes beyond the numbers and includes how you communicate your story. A clear and professional presentation, supported by well-organized documentation and a strong business plan, can significantly enhance your application. Lenders are more likely to approve borrowers who demonstrate preparation, clarity, and confidence.

As you build your borrower profile, it is important to think long-term. The goal is not just to get approved for one loan but to create a financial profile that supports ongoing growth and future opportunities. Each improvement you make strengthens your position for future financing and expands your ability to scale your business and real estate portfolio.

Ultimately, your borrower profile is your foundation. It sets the tone for the entire SBA loan process and influences how every other component is evaluated. By taking control of this aspect of the process, you position yourself for success. You move from being a passive applicant to a strategic borrower who understands how to meet and exceed lender expectations.

This chapter has shown you that approval is not just about meeting minimum requirements—it is about building a strong, well-rounded profile that demonstrates reliability, stability, and capability. As you move forward, you will continue to build on this foundation, learning how to align your business, property, and deal structure with the same level of precision.

Real-Life Math Example: Strengthening a Borrower Profile Through Financial Adjustments

Consider a borrower named Maria who is applying for an SBA commercial mortgage loan to purchase a mixed-use property for $900,000. The lender requires a 10 percent down payment, so Maria needs to contribute $90,000. She currently has $120,000 in savings, which means she will have $30,000 remaining after the down payment. While this meets the minimum requirement, the lender prefers to see at least six months of reserves, which in this case would be approximately $45,000 based on her projected expenses.

Maria's business generates $150,000 in annual net operating income. The proposed loan amount of $810,000 has an annual debt service of approximately $78,000. When calculating the DSCR, the lender divides $150,000 by $78,000, resulting in a ratio of approximately 1.92. This is a strong number and indicates that the business generates nearly double the income needed to cover the loan payments.

However, Maria's credit score is 660, which is acceptable but not ideal. Her credit report shows a few late payments within the past 12 months and a credit card utilization rate of 75 percent. While these factors do not automatically disqualify her, they do increase perceived risk. The lender begins to evaluate whether compensating factors can offset these concerns.

To strengthen her application, Maria decides to take several strategic steps. First, she pays down her credit card balances, reducing her utilization from 75 percent to 30 percent. This improves her credit score to 690 within a short period. This single action significantly improves how her credit profile is perceived. Next, Maria increases her liquidity by securing an additional $20,000 from a business partner who is willing to invest in the project. This raises her total available funds to $140,000. After the $90,000 down payment, she now has $50,000 in reserves, exceeding the lender's preferred threshold. This demonstrates financial stability and reduces risk.

Maria also reviews her business expenses and identifies areas where she can reduce costs. By streamlining operations, she increases her net operating income from $150,000 to $165,000. This improves her DSCR from 1.92 to approximately 2.12, providing an even stronger cushion for the lender.

In addition, Maria prepares a detailed business plan that explains how the mixed-use property will generate additional income through rental units and increased customer traffic.

She includes projections showing how revenue is expected to grow over the next three years. This helps the lender understand the long-term viability of the investment.

Now consider how these changes impact the overall application. Maria's improved credit score, increased reserves, and higher DSCR create a much stronger borrower profile. What was initially a borderline application becomes a highly attractive one. The lender now sees a borrower who has taken proactive steps to reduce risk and strengthen her position. If Maria had not made these adjustments, her application might still have been approved, but with more scrutiny, potential delays, or less favorable terms. By taking control of the variables within her reach, she not only improves her chances of approval but also positions herself for better loan terms and a smoother process.

This example illustrates the power of understanding the borrower profile and making strategic improvements. Small changes in credit utilization, liquidity, and income can have a significant impact on how lenders evaluate risk. More importantly, it shows that borrowers have far more control over the approval process than they often realize.

By applying these principles, you can transform your borrower profile into a strong, compelling case for approval. You can identify weaknesses, implement targeted improvements, and present a complete and well-structured application that aligns with SBA expectations. This is the key to moving from uncertainty to confidence in the SBA loan process.

Chapter 3

Structuring the Deal for Maximum Approval Probability

When it comes to getting approved for an SBA commercial mortgage loan, one of the most powerful and often underestimated factors is how the deal itself is structured. Many borrowers focus heavily on their credit, income, or the property, but overlook the fact that even a strong borrower can be denied if the deal is not structured properly. On the other hand, a well-structured deal can often compensate for minor weaknesses and significantly improve the likelihood of approval. In this chapter, you will learn how to structure your SBA commercial mortgage loan in a way that aligns with lender expectations, minimizes perceived risk, and maximizes your chances of getting approved.

At its core, deal structuring is about creating a balance between risk and reward from the lender's perspective. Every element of the loan—purchase price, down payment, loan amount, use of funds, repayment terms, and collateral—contributes to how the lender evaluates the transaction. The goal is to present a deal that makes logical, financial, and strategic sense. When a lender reviews your file, they should be able to quickly understand why the deal works, how it will generate income, and how the loan will be repaid.

One of the first and most important components of deal structuring is the purchase price and valuation of the property or business. Lenders want to ensure that the price being paid is supported by market data and financial performance. This is typically verified through an appraisal for real estate or a business valuation for acquisitions. If the purchase price is too high relative to the value, it increases risk and can lead to a lower loan amount or even denial. Structuring a deal with a realistic and well-supported purchase price is critical from the beginning.

The down payment is another key factor that plays a major role in approval. SBA loans typically require a minimum of 10 percent down, but contributing more than the minimum can significantly strengthen your application. A larger down payment reduces the loan-to-value ratio, lowers the lender's exposure, and demonstrates your commitment to the deal. It also reduces the monthly payment, which improves the debt service coverage ratio. In many cases, increasing the down payment is one of the simplest and most effective ways to improve a deal.

The loan amount and how it is calculated are equally important. The loan amount should be aligned with both the value of the asset and the income it produces. Borrowers sometimes make the mistake of maximizing the loan amount without considering how it impacts the overall structure. A higher loan amount increases the monthly payment, which can reduce the DSCR and make the deal less attractive to the lender. Structuring the loan at a level that maintains strong cash flow is essential.

Use of funds is another area where clarity and structure are critical. SBA loans allow for a variety of uses, including property acquisition, business purchase, working capital, and renovations. However, lenders want to see that the use of funds is clearly defined and directly supports the success of the business or investment. Vague or overly complex use of funds can create confusion and increase perceived risk. A well-structured deal outlines exactly how the funds will be used and how those uses will contribute to revenue and stability.

Repayment terms also play a significant role in deal structuring. SBA loans typically offer longer terms than conventional commercial loans, which helps reduce monthly payments and improve cash flow. For example, a 25-year amortization on a real estate loan results in lower payments compared to a shorter-term loan. This directly impacts the DSCR and overall affordability of the loan. Choosing the right term is not just about minimizing payments—it is about creating a sustainable financial structure that supports long-term success. Collateral is another important element of the deal. In SBA lending, the primary collateral is often the property being financed, but lenders may also consider additional collateral if needed. The goal is to ensure that the loan is adequately secured. While SBA loans are more flexible with collateral than traditional loans, a strong collateral position still improves approval odds. Understanding how collateral is evaluated and how to strengthen this aspect of your deal can make a significant difference.

Another critical component of deal structuring is aligning the transaction with SBA guidelines. Each SBA program has specific requirements regarding occupancy, use of funds, and borrower eligibility. For example, many SBA real estate loans require that the property be at least 51 percent owner-occupied. Failing to meet these requirements can result in immediate denial, regardless of how strong the rest of the deal is. Ensuring compliance from the beginning is essential.

Seller concessions and creative structuring can also play a role in improving a deal. In some cases, sellers may be willing to carry a portion of the financing or contribute toward closing costs. This can reduce the amount of cash required from the borrower and improve liquidity. However, these structures must be carefully designed to comply with SBA guidelines. When used correctly, they can enhance the overall strength of the deal.

Another powerful strategy in deal structuring is focusing on cash flow optimization. Since DSCR is one of the most important metrics in SBA underwriting, structuring the deal to maximize cash flow is critical. This can include negotiating a better purchase price, increasing the down payment, or selecting loan terms that reduce the monthly payment. Every adjustment that improves cash flow makes the deal more attractive to the lender.

It is also important to consider the timing of the transaction. Market conditions, interest rates, and business performance can all impact how a deal is perceived. Structuring a deal at the right time, when financials are strong and conditions are favorable, can improve approval odds. While timing cannot always be controlled, being aware of its impact allows you to make more informed decisions.

Another key concept is simplicity. Lenders prefer deals that are straightforward and easy to understand. Overly complex structures, multiple entities, or unclear relationships can create confusion and delay the process. A clean and simple deal structure reduces friction and builds confidence. This does not mean that complex deals cannot be approved, but they require a higher level of clarity and documentation. As you structure your deal, it is important to think from the lender's perspective. Ask yourself whether the deal makes sense, whether the numbers are realistic, and whether the risk is justified. This mindset allows you to identify potential issues before they become obstacles. It also helps you present your deal in a way that aligns with how lenders evaluate risk.

Ultimately, deal structuring is about control. While you cannot control every aspect of the approval process, you have significant control over how your deal is presented and structured. By making strategic decisions and aligning your deal with SBA guidelines, you can dramatically increase your chances of approval.

This chapter has shown you that approval is not just about qualifying—it is about positioning. A well-structured deal tells a clear and compelling story that reduces risk and builds confidence. As you move forward, you will continue to refine this approach, learning how to adjust variables and optimize every component of your transaction.

Real-Life Math Example: Structuring an SBA Deal for Approval

Consider a borrower named James who is purchasing a commercial property for $1,500,000 to operate his expanding logistics business. He initially plans to put down the minimum 10 percent, which is $150,000, resulting in a loan amount of $1,350,000. The loan has an interest rate of 7.25 percent with a 25-year amortization, leading to an annual debt service of approximately $115,000.

James's business generates a net operating income of $140,000 per year. When calculating the DSCR, the lender divides $140,000 by $115,000, resulting in a ratio of approximately 1.22. This is slightly below the typical minimum requirement of 1.25, which puts the deal at risk of denial.

To improve the deal, James explores several structuring options. First, he considers increasing his down payment. By increasing his down payment to $250,000, the loan amount is reduced to $1,250,000. This lowers the annual debt service to approximately $107,000. Recalculating the DSCR, $140,000 divided by $107,000 results in a ratio of approximately 1.31. This now meets the lender's requirement and strengthens the deal.

Next, James negotiates the purchase price with the seller and successfully reduces it to $1,450,000. With the same $250,000 down payment, the new loan amount becomes $1,200,000. This further reduces the annual debt service to approximately $102,000. The new DSCR is $140,000 divided by $102,000, which equals approximately 1.37. This creates an even stronger cash flow position.

James also reviews his business operations and identifies ways to increase efficiency. By reducing expenses and improving processes, he increases his net operating income from $140,000 to $155,000. With the updated loan structure, the DSCR becomes $155,000 divided by $102,000, resulting in approximately 1.52. This provides a significant cushion and makes the deal highly attractive to the lender.

Additionally, James works with the seller to include a small seller concession of $20,000 toward closing costs. This allows him to preserve more of his cash reserves, improving his liquidity after closing. Strong reserves further reduce risk and strengthen the overall application.

Now consider the transformation of the deal. Initially, the DSCR was below the required threshold, and the deal was at risk of denial. Through strategic adjustments—higher down payment, negotiated purchase price, increased income, and improved liquidity—James turns the deal into a strong approval candidate.

If James had not made these changes, the lender might have required additional conditions, such as a larger down payment or additional collateral, or could have denied the application altogether. By understanding how each variable impacts the overall structure, James was able to take control of the process and create a deal that aligns with lender expectations.

This example demonstrates that deal structuring is not static. It is dynamic and flexible, allowing you to adjust key variables to improve your position. By focusing on cash flow, reducing risk, and aligning with SBA guidelines, you can transform a borderline deal into a strong one.

The key takeaway is that small changes can have a significant impact. A slight increase in down payment, a modest reduction in purchase price, or a small improvement in income can dramatically improve the DSCR and overall deal strength. When these adjustments are combined, they create a powerful effect that can determine the outcome of your application.

By applying these principles, you gain the ability to design your deal intentionally rather than leaving it to chance. You can identify potential weaknesses, implement targeted improvements, and present a well-structured transaction that meets and exceeds lender expectations. This is the essence of mastering SBA commercial mortgage loan approval.

Chapter 4

Mastering Cash Flow Analysis and Debt Service Coverage for SBA Approval

One of the most critical components of getting approved for an SBA commercial mortgage loan is understanding and mastering cash flow analysis. While credit, experience, and deal structure all play important roles, nothing carries more weight in underwriting than the ability of the business or property to generate enough income to support the loan. Lenders are fundamentally concerned with one question: can this loan be repaid consistently and reliably over time? The answer to that question is found in the numbers, specifically in cash flow and the debt service coverage ratio, commonly referred to as DSCR. In this chapter, you will learn how lenders analyze cash flow, how DSCR is calculated, and how to strategically improve it to maximize your chances of approval.

Cash flow is the lifeblood of any business or income-producing property. It represents the actual money available after all operating expenses have been paid. For SBA loans, lenders focus on net operating income, which is typically calculated by taking gross revenue and subtracting all necessary operating expenses such as payroll, rent, utilities, insurance, and cost of goods sold. However, not all expenses are treated equally in underwriting. Some expenses may be added back to income if they are non-recurring or discretionary, such as certain owner benefits or one-time costs. Understanding these adjustments can significantly impact how your cash flow is presented.

The DSCR is the primary metric used to evaluate whether the cash flow is sufficient. It is calculated by dividing the net operating income by the total annual debt service, which includes both principal and interest payments on the loan. A DSCR of 1.00 means the income exactly equals the debt payments, leaving no margin for error. Most SBA lenders require a minimum DSCR of 1.25, meaning the business generates 25 percent more income than needed to cover the loan. This cushion provides protection for the lender in case of fluctuations in income or unexpected expenses.

Understanding how to calculate DSCR is essential, but more importantly, you must understand how lenders interpret it. A DSCR of 1.25 may meet the minimum requirement, but it is not always considered strong. Higher ratios, such as 1.40 or 1.50, provide greater confidence and can lead to smoother approvals and better terms. Conversely, a DSCR below 1.25 does not automatically mean denial, but it does require compensating factors such as strong reserves, additional collateral, or a larger down payment. Lenders also look at historical cash flow trends. They typically review two to three years of financial statements and tax returns to assess consistency. A business that shows steady or increasing income is viewed more favorably than one with declining or inconsistent performance. Even if the current year is strong, a downward trend in previous years can raise concerns. This is why it is important to present a clear and consistent financial history whenever possible.

Another important aspect of cash flow analysis is normalization. This involves adjusting financial statements to reflect the true earning power of the business. For example, if the owner pays themselves a higher-than-market salary or includes personal expenses in the business, these amounts may be added back to increase the net operating income. Similarly, one-time expenses that are unlikely to recur can also be added back. These adjustments can significantly improve DSCR when properly documented and explained.

Global cash flow is another layer of analysis that lenders consider. This goes beyond the business and includes all sources of income and all obligations of the borrower. For example, if you have additional income from other properties or investments, this can strengthen your application. On the other hand, if you have significant personal debt or obligations, it can reduce your overall cash flow. Lenders want to ensure that your entire financial picture supports the loan, not just the business itself. Seasonality and industry risk are also factors in cash flow analysis. Some businesses experience fluctuations in income depending on the time of year. Lenders take this into account and may look for additional reserves or higher DSCR to offset these risks. Similarly, businesses in more volatile industries may be subject to stricter scrutiny. Understanding how your industry is perceived can help you prepare and present your financials more effectively.

Improving DSCR is one of the most powerful ways to strengthen your SBA loan application. There are several strategies to achieve this. Increasing revenue is the most direct approach, whether through higher sales, expanded services, or improved pricing. Reducing expenses is another effective strategy, as it directly increases net operating income. Even small reductions in recurring expenses can have a significant impact over time.

Another way to improve DSCR is by adjusting the loan structure. Increasing the down payment reduces the loan amount and lowers the monthly payment, which improves the ratio. Extending the amortization period can also reduce payments, although this must be done within SBA guidelines. Negotiating a lower interest rate, when possible, can further improve cash flow.

It is also important to consider the timing of your application. Applying after a strong financial year or after implementing improvements can significantly enhance your DSCR. Waiting until your financials reflect your best performance can make a meaningful difference in how your application is evaluated.

Documentation and presentation are critical when it comes to cash flow. Lenders rely on financial statements, tax returns, and supporting documents to verify your numbers. Clear, accurate, and well-organized financials build confidence and reduce the likelihood of questions or delays. Providing detailed explanations for any adjustments or anomalies helps create a complete and credible picture.

Another key concept is sustainability. Lenders are not just looking at current cash flow—they are evaluating whether it can be maintained over the life of the loan. This is why they consider factors such as customer concentration, market conditions, and business stability. A business that relies heavily on a single client, for example, may be viewed as higher risk. Diversification and stability are important indicators of long-term success.

Stress testing is another technique lenders may use. This involves evaluating how the business would perform under less favorable conditions, such as a decline in revenue or an increase in expenses. A strong DSCR provides a buffer that helps the business withstand these challenges. This is why exceeding the minimum requirement is always beneficial.

As you can see, cash flow analysis is both an art and a science. It involves understanding the numbers, interpreting them correctly, and presenting them in a way that aligns with lender expectations. By mastering this process, you gain a significant advantage in the SBA loan approval process.

This chapter has shown you that DSCR is not just a number—it is a reflection of the strength and sustainability of your business. By focusing on improving cash flow and structuring your deal to support strong ratios, you can dramatically increase your chances of approval. As you move forward, you will continue to build on this knowledge, learning how to optimize every aspect of your application.

Real-Life Math Example: Improving Cash Flow and DSCR for SBA Approval

Consider a borrower named Anthony who owns a growing restaurant business and wants to purchase a commercial property for $1,000,000. He plans to use an SBA 7(a) loan with a 10 percent down payment of $100,000, resulting in a loan amount of $900,000. The loan has an interest rate of 7.75 percent with a 25-year amortization, leading to an annual debt service of approximately $85,000. Anthony's business generates $600,000 in gross revenue annually. After expenses, his net operating income is $105,000. To calculate the DSCR, the lender divides $105,000 by $85,000, resulting in a ratio of approximately 1.24. This is slightly below the typical minimum requirement of 1.25, making the deal borderline.

Anthony decides to analyze his financials more closely. He identifies several discretionary expenses, including $10,000 in owner-related travel and $5,000 in one-time equipment repairs. These expenses are not expected to continue and can be added back to his net operating income. This increases his adjusted income to $120,000.

Recalculating the DSCR, $120,000 divided by $85,000 results in a ratio of approximately 1.41. This adjustment alone transforms the deal from borderline to strong. However, Anthony continues to look for ways to improve his position further.

He negotiates with the seller and reduces the purchase price to $950,000. With the same 10 percent down payment, the loan amount decreases to $855,000. This reduces the annual debt service to approximately $81,000. Using the adjusted income of $120,000, the new DSCR is approximately 1.48.

Anthony also identifies opportunities to reduce ongoing expenses by renegotiating supplier contracts and improving operational efficiency. These changes increase his net operating income by an additional $10,000, bringing it to $130,000. With the updated loan structure, the DSCR becomes $130,000 divided by $81,000, which equals approximately 1.60.

In addition, Anthony increases his down payment to $150,000 by using additional savings. This reduces the loan amount to $800,000 and lowers the annual debt service to approximately $75,000. With the improved income of $130,000, the DSCR now reaches approximately 1.73.

Now consider the transformation. Initially, Anthony's DSCR was below the required threshold, putting the deal at risk. Through a series of strategic adjustments—adding back expenses, negotiating the purchase price, reducing costs, and increasing the down payment—he significantly improves his cash flow position and DSCR.

If Anthony had not taken these steps, the lender might have required additional conditions or denied the application. By understanding how DSCR works and how to influence it, he was able to take control of the process and create a strong, approvable deal.

This example demonstrates that cash flow is not fixed. It can be analyzed, adjusted, and improved with the right strategies. Small changes in income, expenses, or loan structure can have a significant impact on DSCR and overall deal strength.

By applying these principles, you can evaluate your own financials, identify opportunities for improvement, and present a strong case for approval. This is the power of mastering cash flow analysis in the SBA loan process.

Chapter 5

Documentation, Packaging, and Presenting a Loan File That Gets Approved

One of the most overlooked yet decisive factors in getting approved for an SBA commercial mortgage loan is how the loan file is documented, packaged, and presented to the lender. Many borrowers assume that if they meet the qualifications on paper, approval will naturally follow. However, in reality, even strong borrowers with solid financials can face delays or denials if their documentation is incomplete, inconsistent, or poorly organized. On the other hand, a well-prepared and professionally presented loan package can significantly accelerate the approval process and increase lender confidence. In this chapter, you will learn how to build a complete, compelling, and lender-ready loan file that stands out and gets approved.

The first principle of effective loan packaging is completeness. SBA lenders require a comprehensive set of documents to evaluate every aspect of your application. This typically includes personal and business tax returns, financial statements, bank statements, a personal financial statement, a business plan, and details about the property or business being financed. Each document serves a specific purpose, and missing even one piece can create delays or raise concerns. A complete file demonstrates preparation and professionalism, while an incomplete one signals risk and disorganization.

Accuracy is equally important. All documents must align with each other and tell a consistent story. For example, the income reported on your tax returns should match the figures in your financial statements. Bank statements should support the income and expenses shown in your reports. Any discrepancies, even small ones, can trigger questions and slow down the process. Lenders are trained to look for inconsistencies, and when they find them, they may request additional documentation or clarification. Ensuring that your documents are accurate and consistent from the start can prevent unnecessary complications.

Organization is another key element of a strong loan package. Lenders review dozens of files, and a well-organized file makes their job easier. This can have a direct impact on how quickly your application moves through underwriting. Documents should be clearly labeled, logically grouped, and presented in a professional format. For example, personal documents should be separated from business documents, and financial statements should be organized chronologically. A clean and structured file reflects attention to detail and builds confidence.

One of the most important documents in your loan package is the personal financial statement. This document provides a snapshot of your overall financial position, including assets, liabilities, and net worth. It allows the lender to evaluate your liquidity, leverage, and financial stability. A strong personal financial statement shows sufficient assets, manageable liabilities, and positive net worth. It also supports the concept of global cash flow, which is critical in SBA underwriting.

Business financial statements are equally important. These typically include profit and loss statements, balance sheets, and sometimes cash flow statements. These documents provide insight into the performance and health of your business. Lenders use them to calculate key metrics such as DSCR and to assess trends over time. Well-prepared financial statements that clearly show revenue, expenses, and profitability can significantly strengthen your application.

Tax returns serve as a verification tool for both personal and business income. Lenders rely on them to confirm the accuracy of your financial statements and to evaluate long-term trends. Providing complete and accurate tax returns is essential. Any missing pages, unsigned returns, or discrepancies can delay the process. It is also important to be prepared to explain any significant changes in income or unusual items in your returns.

Bank statements provide insight into your financial behavior and liquidity. Lenders review them to verify income, track cash flow, and ensure that funds for the down payment and reserves are available. They also look for consistency in deposits and spending patterns. Large unexplained deposits or irregular activity can raise questions, so it is important to be prepared to provide explanations if needed.

The business plan is another critical component of your loan package. It tells the story behind the numbers and explains how the loan will be used, how the business will operate, and how the loan will be repaid. A strong business plan includes an overview of the business, market analysis, management team, and financial projections. It should be clear, realistic, and aligned with your financial statements. A well-written business plan can significantly enhance your application by providing context and demonstrating your understanding of the business.

Property-related documents are also essential for SBA commercial mortgage loans. These may include purchase agreements, appraisals, lease agreements, and property financials. Lenders use these documents to evaluate the value, condition, and income potential of the property. Ensuring that these documents are complete and accurate is critical to the approval process.

Another important aspect of loan packaging is addressing potential issues upfront. If there are weaknesses in your application, such as lower credit scores, inconsistent income, or gaps in experience, it is better to acknowledge and explain them proactively rather than waiting for the lender to raise questions. Providing clear and reasonable explanations demonstrates transparency and builds trust.

The way you present your loan package also matters. A professional presentation, whether through a digital file or a structured submission, reflects your seriousness and preparedness. Including a summary or cover letter that outlines the key strengths of your application can help guide the lender's review and highlight the most important points.

Communication plays a key role throughout the process. Being responsive, organized, and proactive in providing additional information can keep your file moving forward. Delays in responding to lender requests can slow down the process and create frustration. On the other hand, timely and complete responses demonstrate professionalism and commitment.

Another important concept is consistency across all aspects of the application. Your financial statements, business plan, and supporting documents should all align and reinforce the same narrative. This consistency builds credibility and reduces the likelihood of questions or concerns. When everything fits together logically, the lender can quickly understand and evaluate your application.

Technology can also be a valuable tool in organizing and presenting your loan package. Using digital platforms to store, organize, and share documents can streamline the process and improve efficiency. Ensuring that your files are easily accessible and well-structured can make a significant difference in how your application is handled.

Preparation is the key to success in this stage of the process. Taking the time to gather, review, and organize your documents before submitting your application can save time and prevent issues later. It also allows you to identify and address any potential problems in advance.

Ultimately, documentation and presentation are about building confidence. Lenders want to feel comfortable that they have all the information they need and that the information is reliable. A strong loan package reduces uncertainty and makes it easier for the lender to approve your application.

This chapter has shown you that getting approved is not just about having the right numbers—it is about presenting those numbers in a clear, complete, and compelling way. By mastering documentation and packaging, you position yourself as a professional borrower who understands the process and is prepared for success.

Real-Life Math Example: Organizing and Presenting Financials for SBA Approval

Consider a borrower named Kevin who is applying for an SBA commercial mortgage loan to purchase a small office building for $800,000. He plans to put down $80,000, resulting in a loan amount of $720,000. The loan has an interest rate of 7.5 percent with a 25-year amortization, leading to an annual debt service of approximately $67,000.

Kevin's business generates $400,000 in annual revenue, with total expenses of $300,000, resulting in a net operating income of $100,000. Based on this, the DSCR is calculated as $100,000 divided by $67,000, which equals approximately 1.49. This is a strong ratio and indicates that the business generates sufficient income to support the loan.

However, when Kevin initially submits his application, his documentation is incomplete. His financial statements do not match his tax returns, and some bank statements are missing. The lender identifies discrepancies and requests additional information. This delays the process and creates uncertainty. Kevin decides to reorganize his loan package. He works with his accountant to reconcile his financial statements with his tax returns, ensuring that all numbers align. He provides complete bank statements showing consistent deposits and sufficient funds for the down payment and reserves. He also prepares a detailed personal financial statement showing a net worth of $500,000 and liquidity of $120,000.

In addition, Kevin creates a business plan that explains how the office building will be used and how it will generate income. He includes projections showing an increase in revenue to $450,000 over the next two years. This supports his ability to maintain and improve his DSCR.

Kevin also identifies a discrepancy in his initial financials where a $10,000 expense was incorrectly categorized. By correcting this, his net operating income increases to $110,000. This improves his DSCR to approximately 1.64.

Now consider the impact of these changes. Initially, Kevin had a strong DSCR but a weak presentation, which created delays and risk. By organizing and aligning his documentation, he transforms his application into a clear and compelling case. The lender can now easily verify the numbers and understand the story behind them.

If Kevin had not addressed these issues, the lender might have continued to request additional information or even questioned the reliability of the financials. By taking control of the documentation process, he reduces uncertainty and builds confidence.

This example demonstrates that presentation matters just as much as the numbers themselves. A strong DSCR and solid financials are important, but they must be supported by accurate, complete, and well-organized documentation. When everything aligns, the approval process becomes much smoother.

By applying these principles, you can ensure that your loan package is not only strong but also easy for the lender to evaluate. This increases your chances of approval and helps you move through the process efficiently.

Chapter 6

Choosing the Right SBA Loan Program and Lender for Approval Success

One of the most strategic decisions you will make in the SBA commercial mortgage loan process is selecting the right loan program and the right lender. Many borrowers assume that all SBA loans are essentially the same, but in reality, there are significant differences between programs, and even greater differences between lenders. Choosing the wrong combination can lead to unnecessary delays, stricter requirements, or even denial, while choosing the right one can streamline the process and dramatically increase your chances of approval. In this chapter, you will learn how to align your deal with the most suitable SBA program and how to select a lender that is best positioned to approve your loan.

The two primary SBA loan programs used for commercial mortgage financing are the SBA 7(a) and the SBA 504 loan programs. Each has its own structure, benefits, and ideal use cases. Understanding the differences between these programs is essential because the way your deal is structured must align with the guidelines of the program you choose. The SBA 7(a) loan is known for its flexibility. It can be used for a wide range of purposes, including purchasing real estate, acquiring a business, refinancing debt, and providing working capital. This flexibility makes it a popular choice for borrowers who need a combination of funding uses.

In contrast, the SBA 504 loan program is specifically designed for real estate and equipment purchases. It typically involves a two-loan structure: one from a conventional lender and another from a Certified Development Company (CDC). The 504 program offers long-term, fixed-rate financing, which can provide stability and predictability for borrowers. However, it is less flexible than the 7(a) program and is generally used for straightforward real estate transactions rather than complex business acquisitions or mixed-use financing needs.

Choosing between these programs depends on your specific goals. If you are purchasing a property and also need working capital or want flexibility in how funds are used, the 7(a) program may be the better option. If your primary goal is to secure long-term, fixed-rate financing for a real estate purchase with lower monthly payments, the 504 program may be more suitable. The key is to match your deal structure with the strengths of the program.

Beyond the program itself, the choice of lender plays an even more critical role. Not all SBA lenders are created equal. Some lenders specialize in certain types of loans, industries, or deal sizes. Others may have more experience with complex transactions or unique borrower profiles. Working with a lender that understands your type of deal can significantly improve your chances of approval. A lender who frequently handles similar transactions will be more comfortable with the structure and more efficient in processing your application.

Lender appetite is an important concept to understand. Each lender has its own risk tolerance and preferences. Some lenders may prefer established businesses with strong financials, while others may be more open to startups or borrowers with less experience. Some may focus on specific industries such as healthcare, manufacturing, or hospitality. Identifying a lender whose appetite aligns with your deal can make a significant difference.

Another important factor is whether the lender is a Preferred Lender Program (PLP) lender. PLP lenders have the authority to make credit decisions on behalf of the SBA, which can significantly speed up the approval process. Working with a PLP lender can reduce delays and provide a smoother experience. Non-PLP lenders, on the other hand, must submit loans to the SBA for approval, which can add time and complexity.

Turnaround time is another consideration when choosing a lender. Some lenders are known for faster processing, while others may have longer timelines. If timing is critical for your transaction, selecting a lender with a reputation for efficiency can be beneficial. However, speed should not come at the expense of quality. It is important to balance speed with expertise and reliability.

Communication and responsiveness are also key factors. A lender who communicates clearly, responds promptly, and provides guidance throughout the process can make a significant difference in your experience. The SBA loan process can be complex, and having a lender who is accessible and supportive can help you navigate challenges more effectively.

Another important consideration is how the lender structures deals. Some lenders may be more flexible with down payments, collateral, or DSCR requirements, while others may adhere strictly to minimum guidelines. Understanding these differences can help you choose a lender that aligns with your financial situation and goals.

Fees and costs are also part of the equation. While SBA loans have standardized fees, lenders may have additional costs or variations in how they structure the loan. It is important to understand the full cost of the loan, including interest rates, fees, and closing costs, to ensure that it aligns with your financial plan. Building relationships with lenders can also be beneficial. A strong relationship can lead to better communication, increased trust, and potentially more favorable terms. Even if you are working with a lender for the first time, approaching the relationship professionally and transparently can set a positive tone.

Another strategic approach is to work with multiple lenders or a broker to explore different options. This can provide insight into how different lenders view your deal and allow you to choose the best fit. However, it is important to manage this process carefully to avoid confusion or conflicting information.

Understanding how lenders evaluate deals within each program is also critical. For example, some lenders may have stricter requirements for DSCR or reserves, while others may place more emphasis on borrower experience or collateral. Knowing these nuances allows you to position your application more effectively.

It is also important to consider the long-term implications of your choice. The loan program and lender you select will impact not only your approval but also your experience over the life of the loan. Factors such as servicing, communication, and flexibility can affect your ability to manage the loan and pursue future opportunities. Preparation is key when approaching lenders. Presenting a well-structured deal and a complete loan package increases your credibility and improves your chances of receiving favorable terms. Lenders are more likely to engage with borrowers who demonstrate preparation and professionalism.

Ultimately, choosing the right SBA loan program and lender is about alignment. It is about matching your goals, your deal, and your financial profile with the right structure and the right partner. When this alignment is achieved, the approval process becomes smoother, faster, and more predictable.

This chapter has shown you that approval is not just about meeting requirements—it is about making strategic choices. By selecting the right program and lender, you position yourself for success and create a strong foundation for your SBA financing journey.

Real-Life Math Example: Comparing SBA 7(a) vs. SBA 504 Loan Structures

Consider a borrower named Lisa who wants to purchase a commercial property for $2,000,000 for her expanding medical practice. She is evaluating two options: an SBA 7(a) loan and an SBA 504 loan.

Under the SBA 7(a) option, Lisa is required to put down 10

percent, which is $200,000. The loan amount is $1,800,000. The interest rate is 7.75 percent with a 25-year amortization, resulting in an annual debt service of approximately $168,000.

Lisa's practice generates a net operating income of $240,000 per year. The DSCR is calculated by dividing $240,000 by $168,000, resulting in approximately 1.43. This is a strong ratio and meets lender requirements.

Now consider the SBA 504 option. This structure includes a 50 percent loan from a bank, a 40 percent loan from a CDC, and a 10 percent down payment. Lisa still contributes $200,000, but the financing is split into two parts: $1,000,000 from the bank and $800,000 from the CDC.

The bank portion has an interest rate of 6.75 percent with a 25-year amortization, while the CDC portion has a fixed rate of 6.25 percent with a 25-year term. The combined annual debt service is approximately $150,000.

Using the same net operating income of $240,000, the DSCR under the 504 structure is $240,000 divided by $150,000, which equals approximately 1.60. This is significantly stronger than the 7(a) option.

Now consider the long-term impact. Under the 7(a) loan, Lisa pays $168,000 annually, while under the 504 loan, she pays

$150,000. This results in annual savings of $18,000. Over 10 years, this amounts to $180,000 in savings, not including potential interest rate fluctuations.

However, the 7(a) loan offers more flexibility. If Lisa needed additional funds for working capital or equipment, the 7(a) loan could accommodate those needs, while the 504 loan is more restrictive.

Now imagine that Lisa's net operating income was lower, at $210,000. Under the 7(a) structure, the DSCR would be $210,000 divided by $168,000, resulting in approximately 1.25, which is borderline. Under the 504 structure, the DSCR would be $210,000 divided by $150,000, resulting in approximately 1.40, which is much stronger.

This demonstrates how choosing the right program can directly impact approval. In this scenario, the 504 loan provides a stronger cash flow position and increases the likelihood of approval, especially if income is slightly lower.

Lisa also considers lender options. One lender offers faster processing but slightly higher fees, while another offers lower fees but a longer timeline. By evaluating these factors, she chooses a lender that balances efficiency and cost.

This example highlights the importance of aligning your deal with the right program and lender. Small differences in structure can have a significant impact on DSCR, cash flow, and overall approval probability.

By understanding these options and how they affect your financials, you can make informed decisions that strengthen your application and position you for long-term success.

Chapter 7

Navigating Underwriting, Conditions, and Final Approval

Once your SBA commercial mortgage loan application has been submitted, documented, and structured correctly, it enters one of the most critical phases of the entire process: underwriting. This is where the lender conducts a detailed and comprehensive review of every aspect of your loan file. Many borrowers mistakenly believe that once they submit their documents, the hard part is over. In reality, underwriting is where the final decision is shaped, risks are analyzed in depth, and conditions are issued that must be satisfied before approval and closing. Understanding how this phase works—and how to navigate it strategically—can make the difference between a smooth approval and a frustrating delay or denial.

Underwriting is essentially the lender's process of verifying and validating everything in your loan file. The underwriter reviews your borrower profile, business financials, cash flow, credit history, property details, and deal structure. They are looking for consistency, accuracy, and alignment with SBA guidelines. Their goal is not to find reasons to deny the loan but to ensure that the loan meets all requirements and that the risk is acceptable. However, any inconsistencies, missing information, or unclear elements can trigger questions or additional requirements.

One of the first things underwriters focus on is confirming the numbers. They will recalculate your income, expenses, and DSCR using their own methods and guidelines. This includes reviewing tax returns, financial statements, and any adjustments or add-backs. If your submitted numbers differ from their calculations, they will seek clarification. This is why it is critical that your financials are accurate and well-supported from the beginning.

Another key area of focus is credit analysis. The underwriter reviews your credit report in detail, looking for patterns, trends, and potential risks. They evaluate not only your score but also your payment history, outstanding debts, and any negative items. If there are concerns, such as recent late payments or high utilization, the underwriter may issue conditions requiring explanations or corrective actions.

Cash flow analysis is revisited during underwriting with even greater scrutiny. The underwriter will evaluate both business and global cash flow to ensure that the loan is sustainable. They may stress test the numbers to see how the business would perform under less favorable conditions. If the DSCR is close to the minimum threshold, they may require additional support, such as higher reserves or a larger down payment.

The property is also carefully reviewed. The appraisal is analyzed to confirm the value and condition of the property. Any issues identified in the appraisal, such as deferred maintenance or environmental concerns, may result in conditions that must be addressed before closing. The underwriter also ensures that the property meets SBA occupancy requirements and is suitable for the intended use.

One of the most important aspects of underwriting is the issuance of conditions. Conditions are specific requirements that must be met before the loan can move forward. These can range from simple document requests to more complex requirements such as additional financial information, updated statements, or explanations of certain items. Conditions are not necessarily negative—they are a normal part of the process. However, how you respond to them can significantly impact the timeline and outcome of your loan.

There are typically two types of conditions: prior-to-approval conditions and prior-to-closing conditions. Prior-to-approval conditions must be satisfied before the loan can receive final credit approval. Prior-to-closing conditions are requirements that must be met before the loan can be funded.

Understanding the difference helps you prioritize your responses and manage the process effectively.

Responding to conditions quickly and thoroughly is essential. Delays in providing requested information can slow down the process and create frustration for both you and the lender. Incomplete or unclear responses can lead to additional questions and further delays. The goal is to provide complete, accurate, and well-organized responses that address the condition fully the first time.

Communication during underwriting is critical. Staying in regular contact with your lender or loan officer ensures that you are aware of any updates or additional requirements. It also allows you to address issues proactively rather than reactively. A collaborative approach can help keep the process moving forward smoothly.

Another important concept is maintaining stability during underwriting. Lenders expect your financial situation to remain consistent throughout the process. Major changes, such as taking on new debt, changing jobs, or making large financial transactions, can impact your application and potentially jeopardize approval. It is important to avoid significant changes until the loan has closed.

Transparency is also key during this phase. If there are issues or changes that cannot be avoided, it is better to communicate them openly rather than allowing the lender to discover them later. Honesty and clarity build trust and allow the lender to work with you to find solutions.

As conditions are cleared and the underwriter becomes satisfied with the file, the loan moves toward final approval. This is often referred to as a commitment or approval letter, which outlines the terms and conditions of the loan. While this is a significant milestone, it is not the final step. There are still closing conditions that must be met before funding.

The closing process involves finalizing all documents, verifying information, and ensuring that all conditions have been satisfied. This may include obtaining insurance, finalizing legal documents, and confirming that all funds are in place. Attention to detail during this stage is critical to avoid last-minute issues.

One of the most important strategies for success in underwriting is anticipation. By understanding what underwriters look for and preparing your file accordingly, you can minimize conditions and streamline the process. This includes ensuring that your financials are accurate, your documentation is complete, and your story is consistent.

Another strategy is to view conditions as opportunities rather than obstacles. Each condition is a chance to strengthen your file and provide additional clarity. By approaching them with a proactive and positive mindset, you can turn potential challenges into strengths.

Ultimately, underwriting is about validation. It is the process that confirms that your application meets all requirements and that the loan is a sound investment for the lender. By understanding how this process works and how to navigate it effectively, you can move through it with confidence and control.

This chapter has shown you that approval is not a single event but a process that requires attention, responsiveness, and strategy. By mastering underwriting and conditions, you position yourself to achieve final approval and move successfully to closing.

Real-Life Math Example: Navigating Underwriting Conditions and Adjustments

Consider a borrower named Daniel who is applying for an SBA commercial mortgage loan to purchase a warehouse for $1,300,000. He plans to put down $130,000, resulting in a loan amount of $1,170,000. The loan has an interest rate of 7.5

percent with a 25-year amortization, leading to an annual debt service of approximately $105,000.

Daniel's business generates a net operating income of $135,000 per year. Based on this, the initial DSCR is calculated as $135,000 divided by $105,000, which equals approximately 1.29. This meets the minimum requirement but is not particularly strong, which means the underwriter will likely review the file carefully.

During underwriting, the underwriter recalculates Daniel's income and identifies that $10,000 of the reported income is from a one-time contract that is not expected to continue. This reduces the adjusted net operating income to $125,000. The revised DSCR becomes $125,000 divided by $105,000, which equals approximately 1.19. This falls below the required threshold, triggering a condition.

The lender issues a condition requesting additional support to strengthen the file. Daniel must now find a way to improve the DSCR or provide compensating factors. He reviews his financials and identifies $8,000 in discretionary expenses that can be added back, such as non-essential travel and owner-related costs. This increases his adjusted income to $133,000.

Recalculating the DSCR, $133,000 divided by $105,000 results in approximately 1.27, bringing the ratio back above the minimum requirement. However, the underwriter still considers the deal somewhat tight and requests additional reserves as a compensating factor. Daniel responds by increasing his down payment from $130,000 to $180,000, reducing the loan amount to $1,120,000. This lowers the annual debt service to approximately $100,000. With the adjusted income of $133,000, the new DSCR becomes $133,000 divided by $100,000, which equals 1.33. This provides a stronger cushion and satisfies the underwriter's concerns.

Additionally, Daniel provides updated bank statements showing that he will have $70,000 in reserves after closing. This further strengthens the application by demonstrating financial stability.

Now consider the transformation. Initially, Daniel's DSCR was acceptable but weak. After underwriting adjustments, it dropped below the required level, putting the deal at risk. Through strategic responses—adding back expenses, increasing the down payment, and improving reserves—Daniel was able to strengthen the deal and meet the lender's requirements.

If Daniel had not responded effectively to the conditions, the loan could have been denied. Instead, by understanding how underwriting works and taking proactive steps, he was able to navigate the process successfully.

This example illustrates the importance of flexibility and responsiveness during underwriting. The numbers are not always final when the application is submitted. They can change based on the underwriter's analysis, and your ability to adapt is critical.

By understanding how to interpret and respond to conditions, you can maintain control of the process and guide your loan toward approval. This is the key to successfully navigating the underwriting phase of an SBA commercial mortgage loan.

Chapter 8

Closing the Loan, Funding the Deal, and Positioning for Long-Term Success

Reaching the final stages of an SBA commercial mortgage loan is a major milestone, but it is not the finish line—it is the beginning of execution. After underwriting approval and condition clearance, the loan moves into closing, funding, and post-closing performance. Many borrowers assume that once they receive an approval, everything is complete, but this final phase requires just as much attention to detail, organization, and strategic thinking as the earlier stages. In this chapter, you will learn how to navigate closing efficiently, avoid last-minute issues, and position yourself for long-term financial success after funding.

The closing phase begins once the lender issues a formal commitment or approval letter outlining the terms and conditions of the loan. This document includes the loan amount, interest rate, repayment terms, required insurance, and any remaining conditions that must be satisfied before funding. It is critical to review this document carefully and ensure that all terms align with your expectations. Any discrepancies should be addressed immediately to avoid complications later in the process.

One of the most important aspects of closing is satisfying final conditions. These may include updated financial statements, proof of insurance, verification of funds for the down payment, and completion of legal documentation. While many of these items may seem straightforward, delays often occur when borrowers underestimate the time required to gather and verify this information. Being proactive and organized at this stage can prevent last-minute issues that could delay closing.

The legal component of closing is another critical element. SBA loans involve a significant amount of documentation, including loan agreements, security instruments, guarantees, and other legal forms. These documents must be reviewed, executed, and sometimes notarized. Working with experienced professionals, such as attorneys or closing agents, can help ensure that everything is completed correctly and efficiently. Errors or omissions in legal documents can cause delays or even require re-execution.

Funding the loan involves the transfer of funds from the lender to the appropriate parties, including the seller, escrow accounts, and any other stakeholders involved in the transaction. This process must be carefully coordinated to ensure that all conditions have been met and that funds are disbursed accurately. Understanding how the funding process works allows you to anticipate timing and ensure that all parties are aligned.

One of the most important financial aspects of closing is the verification of funds. Lenders will require proof that you have the necessary funds for the down payment, closing costs, and reserves. These funds must be documented and sourced according to SBA guidelines. Any large or unusual deposits must be explained, and all funds must be verifiable. Ensuring that your funds are properly documented and accessible is essential for a smooth closing.

Closing costs are another key consideration. These can include lender fees, SBA fees, appraisal costs, legal fees, and other expenses associated with the transaction. Understanding these costs in advance allows you to plan accordingly and avoid surprises. While SBA loans offer favorable terms, the upfront costs can be significant, and proper planning is essential.

Insurance requirements are also part of the closing process. Lenders typically require property insurance, and in some cases, additional coverage such as liability or flood insurance. These policies must be in place before funding can occur. Working with an insurance provider early in the process can help ensure that all requirements are met on time.

Once all conditions have been satisfied and documents have been executed, the loan moves to funding. This is the point at which the transaction is completed, and ownership of the property or business is transferred. While this is an exciting moment, it is important to remain focused and ensure that all final details are handled correctly.

After funding, the focus shifts to managing the loan and ensuring long-term success. This includes making timely payments, maintaining strong financial performance, and adhering to any covenants or requirements outlined in the loan agreement. The habits and strategies you implement after closing are just as important as those used to secure the loan.

Cash flow management becomes critical once the loan is in place. Ensuring that your business or property generates sufficient income to cover expenses and loan payments is essential. This requires ongoing monitoring of revenue, expenses, and profitability. By maintaining strong cash flow, you not only meet your obligations but also position yourself for future growth.

Building reserves is another important post-closing strategy. Even if you meet the minimum reserve requirements at closing, continuing to build additional reserves provides a safety net for unexpected challenges. This financial cushion can help you navigate fluctuations in income or unforeseen expenses without jeopardizing your loan. Another key aspect of long-term success is maintaining a strong relationship with your lender. Open communication, timely payments, and transparency can build trust and create opportunities for future financing. A positive relationship with your lender can be a valuable asset as you expand your portfolio or pursue additional investments.

Monitoring your financial performance is also essential. Regularly reviewing your financial statements and key metrics, such as DSCR, allows you to identify trends and make adjustments as needed. Staying proactive in managing your finances helps ensure that you remain in a strong position throughout the life of the loan.

Growth and scalability should also be part of your long-term strategy. The goal of securing an SBA loan is not just to complete a single transaction but to create a foundation for future opportunities. By reinvesting profits, improving operations, and expanding strategically, you can leverage your initial success to achieve greater financial goals.

Risk management is another important consideration. This includes identifying potential risks, such as market changes, economic conditions, or operational challenges, and developing strategies to mitigate them. Being prepared for potential challenges allows you to respond effectively and maintain stability. Refinancing opportunities may also arise over time. As interest rates change or your financial position improves, you may have the option to refinance your loan to achieve better terms or lower payments. Understanding when and how to refinance can provide additional financial benefits.

Another important aspect is compliance with SBA and lender requirements. This may include providing periodic financial statements, maintaining insurance coverage, and adhering to any covenants. Staying compliant ensures that your loan remains in good standing and avoids potential issues.

Ultimately, closing the loan is just the beginning of a larger journey. It represents the transition from planning and preparation to execution and growth. By approaching this phase with the same level of discipline and strategy, you can maximize the benefits of your SBA loan and achieve long-term success.

This chapter has shown you that the final steps of the SBA loan process are just as important as the initial ones. By managing closing, funding, and post-closing performance effectively, you can turn your approved loan into a powerful tool for growth and financial stability.

Real-Life Math Example: Closing, Funding, and Long-Term Financial Performance

Consider a borrower named Steven who has been approved for an SBA commercial mortgage loan to purchase a retail property for $1,100,000. He contributes a 10 percent down payment of $110,000, resulting in a loan amount of $990,000. The loan has an interest rate of 7.25 percent with a 25-year amortization, leading to an annual debt service of approximately $90,000.

Steven's business generates a net operating income of $135,000 per year. At closing, his DSCR is calculated as $135,000 divided by $90,000, which equals 1.50. This is a strong ratio and indicates that the business generates 50 percent more income than required to cover the loan payments.

In addition to the down payment, Steven incurs closing costs totaling $35,000, including SBA fees, appraisal costs, and legal expenses. He starts with $200,000 in savings, uses $145,000 for the down payment and closing costs, and is left with $55,000 in reserves after closing.

After funding, Steven focuses on improving his business operations. Within the first year, he increases revenue by 10 percent, raising his net operating income from $135,000 to

$148,500. With the same annual debt service of $90,000, his DSCR improves to approximately 1.65. Steven also reduces expenses by renegotiating supplier contracts, saving $8,500 annually. This increases his net operating income to $157,000. The new DSCR becomes $157,000 divided by $90,000, which equals approximately 1.74.

Over the next three years, Steven continues to grow his business and increase profitability. His net operating income reaches $180,000. With the same loan payment, his DSCR rises to 2.00, meaning he generates twice the income needed to cover the debt.

At this point, Steven explores refinancing options. Interest rates have decreased, and he is able to refinance his loan at 6.25 percent, reducing his annual debt service to approximately $80,000. With a net operating income of $180,000, his DSCR increases to 2.25.

This improvement in cash flow allows Steven to reinvest in his business and expand to a second location. His strong financial performance and payment history make it easier to secure additional financing.

Now consider the impact of poor post-closing management. If Steven had not increased revenue or reduced expenses, his DSCR would have remained at 1.50. While still acceptable, it would not provide the same level of financial flexibility or growth potential.

If his income had decreased to $110,000 due to poor management, his DSCR would drop to approximately 1.22, putting him at risk of financial strain. This highlights the importance of maintaining and improving cash flow after closing.

This example demonstrates that closing the loan is just the beginning. The real success comes from how you manage the loan and your business over time. By focusing on growth, efficiency, and financial discipline, you can turn your SBA loan into a powerful tool for long-term success.

By applying these principles, you can ensure that your investment not only meets your immediate goals but also creates opportunities for future growth and financial stability.

Chapter 9

SBA Loan Requirements, Interest Rates, and Structuring the Optimal Loan Terms

As you progress deeper into mastering SBA commercial mortgage financing, one of the most important areas to understand is how loan requirements, interest rates, and loan structures all work together to influence approval, affordability, and long-term profitability. Many borrowers focus only on getting approved, but the true advantage comes from understanding how to structure the loan in a way that maximizes cash flow, minimizes risk, and aligns with long-term financial goals. In this chapter, you will learn how SBA loan requirements are applied, how interest rates are determined, and how to strategically structure your loan terms for optimal results.

SBA loan requirements are designed to ensure that borrowers meet minimum standards of creditworthiness, financial stability, and business viability. These requirements include factors such as credit score, DSCR, down payment, liquidity, and borrower experience. While these are often presented as fixed thresholds, there is flexibility within the system. Lenders evaluate the overall strength of the application rather than relying on a single metric. This means that a borrower who is slightly below one requirement may still be approved if other aspects of the application are strong.

Interest rates are one of the most critical components of any loan because they directly impact monthly payments and total cost over time. SBA loan rates are typically tied to a benchmark, such as the prime rate, plus a lender-specific spread. The exact rate you receive depends on factors such as your credit profile, the strength of your financials, the loan amount, and the perceived risk of the transaction. Even small differences in interest rates can have a significant impact on cash flow and long-term costs.

Loan term and amortization are equally important. SBA loans often offer longer amortization periods, such as 20 to 25 years for real estate, which reduces monthly payments and improves cash flow. However, longer terms also result in more interest paid over time. Balancing affordability with total cost is a key part of structuring the optimal loan.

Another critical factor is whether the loan has a fixed or variable interest rate. SBA 504 loans typically offer fixed rates, providing stability and predictability. SBA 7(a) loans, on the other hand, often have variable rates, which can fluctuate over time. Understanding how these rate structures impact your payments is essential for long-term planning.

Prepayment penalties are another aspect of loan structure that borrowers must consider. Many SBA loans include penalties for paying off the loan early, particularly in the first few years. While this may not seem important initially, it can impact your flexibility if you plan to refinance or sell the property in the future. Understanding these terms allows you to make informed decisions.

Loan covenants and requirements also play a role in structuring. These may include maintaining certain financial ratios, providing periodic financial statements, or meeting occupancy requirements. These conditions are designed to protect the lender but must be managed carefully to ensure compliance.

One of the most powerful strategies in structuring SBA loans is optimizing the balance between loan amount and down payment. While the minimum down payment may be 10 percent, increasing it can reduce the loan amount, lower payments, and improve DSCR. This not only increases the likelihood of approval but also enhances long-term financial stability. Another important consideration is the impact of fees. SBA loans include guarantee fees, lender fees, and closing costs. While these are often financed into the loan, they still contribute to the overall cost. Understanding how fees are structured and how they impact your loan allows you to plan more effectively.

The relationship between DSCR and loan structure cannot be overstated. Every decision—interest rate, term, loan amount—affects the DSCR. By adjusting these variables, you can significantly improve your financial position. This is why structuring is not just about meeting requirements but about optimizing the entire financial picture.

Another key concept is sensitivity analysis. This involves evaluating how changes in interest rates, income, or expenses impact your loan. For example, if interest rates increase, how does that affect your payment and DSCR? If income decreases, can you still cover your obligations? Understanding these scenarios helps you prepare for potential risks.

Timing can also influence loan terms. Interest rates fluctuate based on market conditions, and applying at the right time can result in more favorable terms. While timing cannot always be controlled, being aware of market trends can help you make better decisions.

Negotiation is another important aspect of structuring. While SBA guidelines set certain parameters, there may be room to negotiate aspects such as interest rate, fees, or terms. Working with experienced lenders and understanding your leverage can lead to better outcomes.

Long-term planning should always be part of your strategy. The loan you choose today will impact your financial position for years to come. Structuring a loan that supports growth, flexibility, and stability is essential for achieving your goals.

Risk management is also a key consideration. This includes preparing for potential changes in income, expenses, or market conditions. Structuring your loan with a margin of safety, such as a higher DSCR or additional reserves, can help mitigate these risks.

Ultimately, structuring the optimal SBA loan is about alignment. It is about aligning your financial goals with the terms of the loan, ensuring that the structure supports both approval and long-term success. By understanding how each component interacts, you can make informed decisions that benefit you over time.

This chapter has shown you that the loan itself is a powerful tool. When structured correctly, it can enhance cash flow, reduce risk, and support growth. As you continue your journey, this knowledge will allow you to approach SBA financing with confidence and precision.

Real-Life Math Example: Comparing Loan Structures and Interest Rate Impact

Consider a borrower named Rachel who is purchasing a commercial property for $1,400,000. She is evaluating two SBA 7(a) loan options with different interest rates and structures.

Option 1: Rachel puts down 10 percent, or $140,000, resulting in a loan amount of $1,260,000. The interest rate is 7.75 percent with a 25-year amortization. The annual debt service is approximately $115,000.

Option 2: Rachel decides to increase her down payment to $200,000, reducing the loan amount to $1,200,000. She also secures a slightly lower interest rate of 7.25 percent due to her stronger financial profile. The annual debt service for this option is approximately $105,000.

Rachel's business generates a net operating income of $170,000 per year. Under Option 1, the DSCR is $170,000 divided by $115,000, which equals approximately 1.48. Under Option 2, the DSCR is $170,000 divided by $105,000, which equals approximately 1.62.

Now consider the long-term impact. Under Option 1, Rachel pays $115,000 annually, while under Option 2, she pays $105,000. This results in annual savings of $10,000. Over 10 years, this amounts to $100,000 in savings. If interest rates were to increase by 1 percent in a variable-rate scenario, Rachel's annual debt service under Option 1 could rise to approximately $125,000, reducing her DSCR to approximately 1.36. Under Option 2, the payment might increase to $115,000, resulting in a DSCR of approximately 1.48. This demonstrates how a stronger initial structure provides a buffer against rate increases.

Now consider a scenario where Rachel's income decreases to $150,000 due to market conditions. Under Option 1, the DSCR would be $150,000 divided by $115,000, which equals approximately 1.30. Under Option 2, the DSCR would be $150,000 divided by $105,000, which equals approximately 1.43. Again, the stronger structure provides greater stability.

Rachel also evaluates the total cost of each loan over time. While Option 2 requires a higher upfront investment, it results in lower interest costs due to the reduced loan amount and lower rate. This improves her overall financial position.

This example demonstrates how small changes in loan structure—such as down payment and interest rate—can have a significant impact on cash flow, DSCR, and long-term costs. By understanding these relationships, Rachel is able to choose the option that best aligns with her goals. If Rachel had focused only on minimizing her upfront investment, she might have chosen Option 1 without considering the long-term implications. By analyzing the numbers and understanding the impact of each variable, she makes a more informed decision.

This example highlights the importance of strategic structuring. The goal is not just to get approved but to create a loan that supports long-term success. By applying these principles, you can optimize your loan terms and position yourself for growth and stability.

Chapter 10

Advanced SBA Commercial Mortgage Loan Structuring and Scaling Your Portfolio

As you reach the final stage of this series, the focus shifts from simply getting approved for an SBA commercial mortgage loan to mastering advanced structuring strategies that allow you to scale, optimize, and build long-term wealth. By now, you understand the fundamentals of borrower qualification, cash flow analysis, deal structuring, documentation, underwriting, and loan terms. This chapter brings all of those elements together and elevates your approach to a higher level—one where you are not just completing transactions, but strategically designing them to maximize growth, efficiency, and long-term financial leverage.

Advanced structuring begins with understanding that each deal is part of a larger portfolio strategy. Instead of evaluating each loan in isolation, you begin to consider how each property, business, and loan interacts with your overall financial picture. This includes how each acquisition impacts your global cash flow, your liquidity, your borrowing capacity, and your long-term goals. The objective is to create a system where each deal strengthens your ability to complete the next one.

One of the most powerful strategies in advanced SBA structuring is leveraging cash flow across multiple assets. As you acquire additional properties or businesses, the combined income from these assets can support larger and more complex transactions. This is where global cash flow becomes a strategic tool rather than just an underwriting requirement. By maintaining strong performance across your portfolio, you create a foundation that allows you to qualify for additional financing.

Another key concept is recycling capital. After acquiring a property and improving its performance, you may have the opportunity to refinance or extract equity. This capital can then be reinvested into new opportunities. While SBA loans have certain restrictions on refinancing and equity extraction, understanding how and when to reposition your assets can create significant growth opportunities over time.

Portfolio diversification is another important strategy. Relying on a single type of property or business can increase risk. By diversifying across different asset types, industries, or locations, you reduce exposure to any single risk factor. This not only strengthens your overall portfolio but can also improve how lenders view your financial stability. Another advanced strategy is layering income streams within a single property or business. For example, a commercial property may include multiple tenants, each contributing to the overall cash flow. This diversification within a single asset can improve stability and increase DSCR. Similarly, businesses that generate revenue from multiple sources are often viewed as lower risk.

Structuring for scalability also involves managing your debt strategically. While SBA loans provide favorable terms, it is important to ensure that your debt levels remain manageable. This includes maintaining strong DSCR across your portfolio and avoiding over-leveraging. Strategic use of debt allows you to grow while maintaining financial stability.

Another important concept is timing your acquisitions. Market conditions, interest rates, and business performance all influence the success of a deal. Advanced borrowers pay close attention to these factors and time their transactions to maximize opportunities. While timing cannot always be perfect, being aware of market trends allows you to make more informed decisions.

Building a strong financial foundation is essential for scaling. This includes maintaining reserves, managing cash flow, and ensuring that each asset performs as expected. Strong financial management not only supports current operations but also positions you for future growth.

Another key strategy is building relationships with lenders. As you complete successful transactions and demonstrate reliability, lenders become more comfortable working with you. This can lead to faster approvals, better terms, and increased flexibility in future deals. A strong track record is one of your most valuable assets.

Advanced structuring also involves understanding how to position deals creatively within SBA guidelines. This may include combining real estate and business acquisitions, structuring seller financing, or optimizing the use of funds. While creativity is important, it must always align with SBA requirements to ensure approval.

Risk management becomes even more critical as you scale. This includes identifying potential risks, such as market fluctuations, tenant turnover, or changes in business performance, and developing strategies to mitigate them. Maintaining a margin of safety in your deals, such as higher DSCR or additional reserves, helps protect your portfolio.

Another important aspect is operational efficiency. As your portfolio grows, managing multiple properties or businesses becomes more complex. Implementing systems and processes to streamline operations can improve performance and reduce risk. This includes financial management, tenant relations, and maintenance.

Long-term planning is at the core of advanced structuring. This involves setting clear goals for your portfolio, such as income targets, asset growth, or geographic expansion. Each deal should align with these goals and contribute to your overall strategy.

Another powerful concept is compounding growth. As you reinvest profits and leverage your existing assets, your portfolio can grow exponentially over time. This requires discipline, patience, and a clear strategy, but the results can be significant.

Exit strategies are also an important consideration. Whether you plan to hold assets long-term, sell them for profit, or refinance, having a clear exit strategy allows you to make better decisions. Understanding how each deal fits into your long-term plan ensures that you remain focused and strategic.

Technology and data analysis can also play a role in advanced structuring. Using tools to analyze market trends, property performance, and financial metrics can provide valuable insights and improve decision-making.

Ultimately, advanced SBA loan structuring is about control and vision. It is about moving from a transactional mindset to a strategic one, where each decision is made with a clear understanding of its impact on your overall portfolio.

This chapter represents the culmination of everything you have learned in this series. By applying these advanced strategies, you can move beyond simply getting approved and begin building a scalable, profitable, and resilient commercial real estate and business portfolio.

Real-Life Math Example: Scaling an SBA Portfolio Through Strategic Structuring

Consider an investor named Michael who starts with a single SBA commercial mortgage loan to purchase a property for $1,000,000. He puts down 10 percent, or $100,000, resulting in a loan amount of $900,000. The annual debt service is approximately $85,000. The property generates a net operating income of $130,000, resulting in a DSCR of approximately 1.53.

After two years, Michael improves the property's performance, increasing net operating income to $150,000. His DSCR rises to approximately 1.76. This strong performance positions him to acquire a second property.

Michael purchases a second property for $1,200,000 with a 10 percent down payment of $120,000. The loan amount is $1,080,000, with an annual debt service of approximately $100,000. The property generates a net operating income of $140,000, resulting in a DSCR of 1.40.

Now consider Michael's global cash flow. His combined net operating income from both properties is $150,000 plus $140,000, totaling $290,000. His combined debt service is $85,000 plus $100,000, totaling $185,000. His global DSCR is $290,000 divided by $185,000, which equals approximately 1.57.

With a strong global DSCR, Michael is able to qualify for a third property. He purchases a property for $1,500,000 with a down payment of $150,000 and a loan amount of $1,350,000. The annual debt service is approximately $125,000, and the property generates a net operating income of $175,000, resulting in a DSCR of 1.40.

Now his total portfolio includes three properties. His combined net operating income is $150,000 plus $140,000 plus $175,000, totaling $465,000. His combined debt service is $85,000 plus $100,000 plus $125,000, totaling $310,000. His global DSCR is $465,000 divided by $310,000, which equals approximately 1.50.

Michael continues to improve performance across his portfolio, increasing total net operating income to $500,000. With the same debt service of $310,000, his global DSCR rises to approximately 1.61. At this point, Michael has built a portfolio that generates strong cash flow and supports additional growth. By reinvesting profits and maintaining strong performance, he positions himself to continue scaling.

Now consider the impact of poor structuring. If Michael had over-leveraged his first property with a higher loan amount, his DSCR might have been lower, limiting his ability to qualify for additional loans. Similarly, if his properties generated inconsistent income, his global cash flow would not support expansion.

This example demonstrates the power of strategic structuring and scaling. By maintaining strong DSCR, managing debt, and reinvesting profits, Michael is able to grow his portfolio systematically.

It also highlights the importance of consistency. Each property contributes to the overall strength of the portfolio, and maintaining performance across all assets is essential for continued growth.

By applying these principles, you can move beyond individual transactions and begin building a scalable portfolio that generates consistent income and long-term wealth.

Chapter 11

Avoiding Loan Denials, Fixing Weak Files, and Turning Rejections Into Approvals

No matter how strong your intentions or how promising your deal may seem, not every SBA commercial mortgage loan application gets approved on the first attempt. In fact, one of the defining characteristics of successful borrowers is not that they avoid rejection altogether, but that they understand how to diagnose, fix, and resubmit a file in a way that turns a denial into an approval. This chapter is about mastering that process. It is about understanding why loans get denied, how to identify weaknesses in your application, and how to strategically rebuild your file so that it meets lender expectations.

Loan denials typically occur for a small number of core reasons. These include insufficient cash flow, weak credit, lack of liquidity, poor deal structure, incomplete documentation, or misalignment with SBA guidelines. While these issues may seem significant, they are often fixable with the right approach. The key is to move from a reactive mindset to a diagnostic one. Instead of asking why the loan was denied in a general sense, you must break down each component of the application and identify exactly where the weakness occurred.

One of the most common reasons for denial is insufficient DSCR. If the business or property does not generate enough income to support the loan payments, the lender will view the deal as too risky. However, this does not mean the deal is dead. There are multiple ways to address this issue, such as increasing revenue, reducing expenses, restructuring the loan, or increasing the down payment. Each of these adjustments can improve cash flow and bring the DSCR above the required threshold.

Credit issues are another common cause of denial. Late payments, high utilization, or unresolved collections can raise concerns about a borrower's reliability. The solution is not simply to accept these issues but to take proactive steps to improve them. Paying down balances, resolving negative items, and establishing a consistent payment history can significantly improve your credit profile. Even small improvements can have a meaningful impact on how lenders view your application.

Liquidity is another critical factor. Lenders want to see that you have sufficient funds for the down payment and reserves. A lack of liquidity can signal that you may struggle to handle unexpected expenses. Increasing your available funds, whether through savings, partnerships, or asset liquidation, can strengthen your application and reduce perceived risk.

Deal structure is often an overlooked cause of denial. Even strong borrowers can be denied if the deal is not structured properly. This includes issues such as an inflated purchase price, insufficient down payment, or misaligned use of funds. Restructuring the deal to better align with SBA guidelines can significantly improve approval odds.

Documentation issues can also lead to denial. Missing, inconsistent, or unclear documents create uncertainty for the lender. Ensuring that your documentation is complete, accurate, and well-organized is essential. This includes aligning financial statements with tax returns and providing clear explanations for any discrepancies.

Another important concept is understanding lender feedback. When a loan is denied, the lender typically provides reasons for the decision. This feedback is valuable because it identifies the specific issues that need to be addressed. Instead of viewing it as a setback, you should use it as a roadmap for improvement.

Working with experienced professionals can also help in fixing a weak file. Loan brokers, accountants, and advisors can provide insights and strategies that may not be immediately obvious. Their experience can help you identify weaknesses and implement effective solutions. Timing is another important factor. Some issues, such as credit improvement or financial performance, require time to address. Being patient and allowing your financial profile to improve before reapplying can increase your chances of success. Rushing the process without making meaningful changes often leads to repeated denials.

Another key strategy is strengthening compensating factors. If one area of your application is weak, you can offset it with strengths in other areas. For example, strong liquidity, a higher down payment, or additional collateral can compensate for lower DSCR or credit challenges.

Understanding SBA guidelines is also critical. Some denials occur simply because the deal does not meet specific requirements, such as occupancy rules or use of funds. Ensuring compliance with these guidelines is essential for approval.

Another important concept is persistence. Many successful borrowers have faced multiple denials before achieving approval. The difference is that they learn from each attempt and continuously improve their application. Persistence, combined with strategy, leads to success.

Rebuilding a loan file involves a systematic approach. This includes reviewing the original application, identifying weaknesses, implementing improvements, and presenting a stronger case. Each step should be intentional and aligned with lender expectations.

Another key aspect is presentation. Even after making improvements, how you present your application matters. A clear, organized, and compelling presentation can enhance the perceived strength of your file.

Communication with lenders is also important during this process. Being transparent about previous denials and demonstrating the steps you have taken to address them can build trust and improve your chances of approval.

Ultimately, turning a denial into an approval is about control. It is about taking ownership of the process, understanding the factors that influence the decision, and making strategic adjustments to improve your position.

This chapter has shown you that denial is not the end—it is part of the process. By approaching it with the right mindset and strategy, you can transform setbacks into opportunities and achieve your financing goals.

Real-Life Math Example: Turning a Denied SBA Loan Into an Approved Deal

Consider a borrower named Carlos who applies for an SBA commercial mortgage loan to purchase a property for $1,250,000. He plans to put down $125,000, resulting in a loan amount of $1,125,000. The annual debt service is approximately $105,000.

Carlos's business generates a net operating income of $120,000. The initial DSCR is calculated as $120,000 divided by $105,000, which equals approximately 1.14. This is below the required threshold of 1.25, leading to a denial.

Carlos reviews the lender's feedback and identifies the main issue as insufficient cash flow. He begins by analyzing his financials and identifies $10,000 in discretionary expenses that can be added back. This increases his adjusted income to $130,000.

Recalculating the DSCR, $130,000 divided by $105,000 results in approximately 1.24, which is still slightly below the required level. Carlos then decides to increase his down payment to $175,000, reducing the loan amount to

$1,075,000. This lowers the annual debt service to approximately $100,000.

With the adjusted income of $130,000, the new DSCR becomes $130,000 divided by $100,000, which equals 1.30. This now meets the lender's requirement. Carlos also works on improving his credit score from 650 to 690 by paying down credit card balances and resolving a collection account. This strengthens his borrower profile. In addition, Carlos increases his reserves by securing an additional $25,000 from a partner. This improves his liquidity and provides a cushion for the lender.

With these improvements, Carlos resubmits his application. The lender now sees a stronger DSCR, improved credit, and better liquidity. The deal is approved.

Now consider the transformation. Initially, Carlos's DSCR was too low, and his application was denied. By making targeted adjustments—adding back expenses, increasing the down payment, improving credit, and increasing reserves—he was able to turn a weak file into a strong one.

If Carlos had not taken these steps, he might have continued to face denials. Instead, by understanding the reasons for the denial and addressing them strategically, he achieved approval.

This example demonstrates that loan denials are often the result of specific, identifiable issues that can be corrected. By taking a systematic approach and making targeted improvements, you can significantly increase your chances of success.

It also highlights the importance of persistence and adaptability. The ability to learn from setbacks and adjust your strategy is a key factor in achieving long-term success in SBA financing. By applying these principles, you can approach the loan process with confidence, knowing that even if challenges arise, you have the tools and strategies to overcome them.

Chapter 12

Advanced Risk Management, Market Cycles, and Protecting Your SBA Investments

As you continue to build and scale your portfolio using SBA commercial mortgage loans, one of the most important skills you must develop is the ability to manage risk effectively. While getting approved and closing deals are critical milestones, long-term success depends on your ability to protect your investments through changing market conditions, economic cycles, and operational challenges. In this chapter, you will learn how to identify risks, prepare for market fluctuations, and implement strategies that preserve your capital while allowing for continued growth.

Risk in commercial real estate and business ownership comes in many forms. These include market risk, tenant or customer risk, operational risk, interest rate risk, and liquidity risk. Each of these factors can impact your ability to generate income and meet your loan obligations. Understanding these risks and planning for them is essential to maintaining stability and avoiding financial setbacks. Market cycles are one of the most significant factors affecting your investments. Real estate and business markets move through periods of expansion, peak, contraction, and recovery. During expansion, values increase, demand is strong, and financing is more accessible. At the peak, prices may be high, and competition increases. During contraction, demand may decline, values may drop, and access to financing may tighten. Recovery marks the beginning of a new cycle of growth.

Successful investors do not try to predict these cycles perfectly—they prepare for them. This means structuring deals with enough margin of safety to withstand downturns. A strong DSCR, adequate reserves, and conservative assumptions are key components of this strategy. When your deals are structured with resilience in mind, you are better positioned to navigate challenging periods.

One of the most important tools in risk management is maintaining reserves. Cash reserves act as a buffer against unexpected events, such as temporary declines in income, unexpected expenses, or economic downturns. While lenders may require a minimum level of reserves, building additional reserves beyond this requirement provides greater security and flexibility.

Another critical strategy is diversification. Relying on a single property, tenant, or business increases your exposure to risk.

By diversifying across multiple assets, industries, or income streams, you reduce the impact of any single issue. For example, a portfolio that includes multiple tenants or businesses is less vulnerable to the loss of any one source of income.

Tenant and customer risk is another important consideration. For commercial properties, tenant stability directly impacts cash flow. Long-term leases with reliable tenants provide stability, while short-term or uncertain tenants increase risk. Similarly, businesses that rely heavily on a small number of customers are more vulnerable than those with a diversified customer base. Managing this risk involves careful selection and ongoing monitoring.

Operational efficiency is also a key factor in risk management. Efficient operations reduce costs, improve profitability, and create a stronger financial position. This includes managing expenses, maintaining properties, and optimizing business processes. Strong operations provide a foundation for stability and growth.

Interest rate risk is another factor that can impact SBA loans, particularly those with variable rates. Changes in interest rates can affect your loan payments and overall cash flow. Understanding how rate changes impact your financials and planning accordingly can help mitigate this risk. This may include maintaining higher DSCR or considering refinancing options when appropriate.

Liquidity risk refers to your ability to access cash when needed. Even profitable investments can face challenges if liquidity is insufficient. Maintaining accessible funds and managing cash flow effectively ensures that you can meet obligations and respond to opportunities or challenges.

Stress testing is a powerful tool for managing risk. This involves evaluating how your investments would perform under different scenarios, such as a decrease in income, an increase in expenses, or changes in interest rates. By understanding these scenarios, you can identify potential vulnerabilities and take steps to address them before they become issues.

Another important concept is conservative underwriting. While it may be tempting to assume optimistic growth or minimal expenses, using conservative assumptions provides a more realistic and safer foundation for your deals. This approach reduces the likelihood of unexpected challenges and improves long-term stability.

Monitoring performance is also critical. Regularly reviewing financial statements, occupancy levels, and key metrics allows you to identify trends and address issues early. Proactive management helps prevent small problems from becoming larger ones.

Insurance plays a role in protecting your investments as well. Adequate coverage for property, liability, and other risks ensures that you are protected against unforeseen events. Working with knowledgeable insurance providers can help you identify and address potential gaps in coverage.

Another key aspect of risk management is maintaining flexibility. Being able to adapt to changing conditions, whether through adjusting operations, refinancing, or repositioning assets, allows you to respond effectively to challenges.

Economic awareness is also important. Understanding broader economic trends, such as employment rates, interest rate movements, and industry conditions, provides context for your investments and helps inform your decisions.

Another advanced strategy is building multiple exit options. Having the ability to sell, refinance, or reposition an asset provides flexibility and reduces risk. This ensures that you are not dependent on a single outcome.

Risk management is not about avoiding risk entirely—it is about managing it intelligently. Every investment carries some level of risk, but by understanding and controlling that risk, you can create opportunities for growth while protecting your capital.

As your portfolio grows, risk management becomes increasingly important. The larger your portfolio, the greater the potential impact of any single issue. Implementing strong systems and strategies ensures that your growth remains sustainable.

Ultimately, protecting your investments is about balance. It is about combining growth with stability, opportunity with caution, and ambition with discipline. By mastering these principles, you can build a portfolio that not only grows but endures.

This chapter has shown you that long-term success is not just about acquiring assets—it is about protecting and managing them effectively. By applying these strategies, you can navigate market cycles, mitigate risks, and maintain a strong and resilient portfolio.

Real-Life Math Example: Stress Testing and Protecting an SBA Investment

Consider an investor named Daniel who owns a commercial property purchased for $1,200,000 using an SBA loan. He put down $120,000, resulting in a loan amount of $1,080,000. The annual debt service is approximately $100,000.

The property generates a net operating income of $160,000, resulting in a DSCR of 1.60. This is a strong position and provides a comfortable margin above the minimum requirement.

Daniel decides to perform a stress test to evaluate how his investment would perform under different scenarios. First, he considers a 15 percent decline in income due to market conditions or tenant turnover. This reduces his net operating income from $160,000 to $136,000.

With the same debt service of $100,000, his DSCR becomes $136,000 divided by $100,000, which equals 1.36. While lower, this still remains above the minimum threshold, indicating that the investment can withstand a moderate decline in income.

Next, Daniel considers an increase in expenses of $20,000 due to maintenance or operational costs. This reduces his net operating income to $140,000. His DSCR becomes $140,000 divided by $100,000, which equals 1.40.

He then combines both scenarios—a 15 percent decline in income and a $20,000 increase in expenses. This reduces his net operating income to $116,000. His DSCR becomes $116,000 divided by $100,000, which equals 1.16. This falls below the desired threshold and indicates potential risk.

To mitigate this risk, Daniel increases his reserves to cover six months of debt service, or $50,000. This provides a buffer that allows him to manage temporary challenges without defaulting on the loan.

Daniel also works to diversify his tenant base, reducing reliance on any single tenant. This decreases the likelihood of a significant income drop.

Additionally, he identifies opportunities to increase income by adding new services and improving property management. These changes increase his net operating income to $170,000, raising his DSCR to 1.70.

Now consider the impact of interest rate changes. If his loan has a variable rate and increases by 1 percent, his annual debt service rises to $110,000. With a net operating income of $170,000, his DSCR becomes approximately 1.55, which remains strong.

This example demonstrates how stress testing and proactive management can help identify and mitigate risks. By understanding how different factors impact his investment, Daniel is able to take steps to protect his financial position.

If Daniel had not performed this analysis, he might not have been prepared for potential challenges. By taking a proactive approach, he ensures that his investment remains stable and resilient. This example highlights the importance of planning for uncertainty. While you cannot predict every outcome, you can prepare for a range of scenarios and position yourself to handle them effectively.

By applying these principles, you can protect your investments, maintain strong performance, and continue to grow your portfolio with confidence.

Chapter 13

Building a Repeatable SBA Loan System and Creating Long-Term Financial Freedom

At this stage in your journey, you have developed a deep understanding of how SBA commercial mortgage loans work—from qualification and underwriting to structuring, closing, and scaling. The final step is transforming this knowledge into a repeatable system that allows you to consistently secure funding, grow your portfolio, and build long-term financial freedom. This chapter is about creating that system. It is about moving from individual transactions to a scalable model that can be replicated over time with efficiency, confidence, and increasing success.

A repeatable SBA loan system begins with clarity. You must define your goals and strategy before pursuing additional deals. This includes identifying the types of properties or businesses you want to acquire, the markets you want to operate in, and the financial targets you aim to achieve. Without clear direction, it becomes difficult to evaluate opportunities and make strategic decisions. With clarity, every deal becomes a step toward a larger objective. The next component of a repeatable system is consistency. This involves developing standardized processes for evaluating deals, preparing loan packages, and managing financials. By creating a consistent approach, you reduce variability and improve efficiency. This includes having templates for financial analysis, checklists for documentation, and systems for tracking performance. Consistency allows you to move faster and with greater confidence.

Another critical element is deal flow. To build a scalable system, you need a steady pipeline of opportunities. This requires proactive sourcing through brokers, direct outreach, marketing, and networking. The more opportunities you evaluate, the more selective you can be, allowing you to focus on high-quality deals that meet your criteria. Deal flow is the engine that drives growth.

Financial discipline is also essential. Maintaining strong financials, managing cash flow, and building reserves are foundational to your system. Each deal should contribute to your overall financial strength rather than weaken it. This includes ensuring that each property or business generates positive cash flow and supports your ability to qualify for future financing.

Another key component is leveraging your track record. As you complete successful transactions and build a portfolio, your credibility with lenders increases. This track record becomes a powerful asset that can lead to faster approvals, better terms, and greater flexibility. Documenting your success and presenting it effectively can enhance your ability to secure future loans.

Automation and delegation are also important as your system grows. Managing multiple deals and properties can become complex, and relying solely on manual processes can limit scalability. Implementing systems for financial management, communication, and operations can improve efficiency. Delegating tasks to professionals, such as accountants, property managers, and advisors, allows you to focus on strategy and growth.

Another important aspect of a repeatable system is continuous improvement. Each deal provides valuable insights that can be used to refine your approach. This includes analyzing what worked well, identifying areas for improvement, and adjusting your strategy accordingly. Over time, this process leads to greater efficiency and success.

Risk management is a critical component of any scalable system. As your portfolio grows, so does your exposure to risk.

Identifying potential risks and implementing strategies to mitigate them is essential. This includes maintaining reserves, diversifying your portfolio, and ensuring that each deal has a margin of safety.

Another key strategy is maintaining flexibility. While having a system is important, it is equally important to adapt to changing conditions. Market trends, interest rates, and business environments can shift, and your system must be able to accommodate these changes. Flexibility allows you to take advantage of opportunities and navigate challenges effectively.

Building relationships is another cornerstone of a repeatable system. Strong relationships with lenders, brokers, and industry professionals can provide access to opportunities, insights, and support. These relationships can also enhance your credibility and improve your chances of approval.

Another important concept is scalability. As your system becomes more refined, you should be able to handle larger and more complex deals. This requires not only financial capacity but also operational capability. Scaling effectively involves balancing growth with stability.

Long-term vision is at the heart of this process. Building a portfolio is not just about acquiring assets—it is about creating a sustainable and growing source of income. This requires a clear vision of where you want to be and a plan for how to get there. Each deal should align with this vision and contribute to your long-term goals.

Another powerful concept is compounding. As you reinvest profits and leverage your existing assets, your portfolio can grow exponentially over time. This requires discipline and patience, but the results can be transformative.

Exit strategies are also an important part of your system. Whether you plan to hold assets long-term, sell them for profit, or refinance, having a clear plan allows you to make better decisions. Understanding how each deal fits into your overall strategy ensures that you remain focused and intentional.

Financial independence is the ultimate goal of this process. By building a portfolio that generates consistent cash flow, you can create a level of financial freedom that allows you to pursue your goals and opportunities without relying on traditional income sources.

Another key aspect is legacy building. Beyond financial success, your portfolio can serve as a foundation for future generations. This involves not only building wealth but also creating systems and structures that can be sustained over time.

Ultimately, building a repeatable SBA loan system is about transformation. It is about moving from a transactional mindset to a strategic one, where each decision is made with a clear understanding of its impact on your overall financial future.

This chapter represents the culmination of everything you have learned in this series. By applying these principles, you can create a system that allows you to consistently secure funding, grow your portfolio, and achieve long-term financial freedom.

Real-Life Math Example: Creating a Repeatable SBA Loan System for Portfolio Growth

Consider an investor named Sophia who starts with a single SBA loan to purchase a property for $900,000. She puts down $90,000, resulting in a loan amount of $810,000. The annual debt service is approximately $75,000. The property generates a net operating income of $120,000, resulting in a DSCR of 1.60.

Sophia implements a system for evaluating and managing her investments. She tracks her income, expenses, and cash flow, ensuring that her property performs consistently. After one year, she increases her net operating income to $130,000, improving her DSCR to approximately 1.73.

Using her strong financial performance, Sophia acquires a second property for $1,100,000 with a down payment of $110,000. The loan amount is $990,000, with an annual debt service of approximately $90,000. The property generates a net operating income of $140,000, resulting in a DSCR of 1.56.

Now consider her combined portfolio. Her total net operating income is $130,000 plus $140,000, totaling $270,000. Her total debt service is $75,000 plus $90,000, totaling $165,000. Her global DSCR is $270,000 divided by $165,000, which equals approximately 1.64.

Sophia continues to refine her system, improving efficiency and increasing income. She acquires a third property for $1,300,000 with a down payment of $130,000 and a loan amount of $1,170,000. The annual debt service is approximately $105,000, and the property generates a net operating income of $160,000, resulting in a DSCR of 1.52.

Her total portfolio now includes three properties with a combined net operating income of $430,000 and total debt service of $270,000. Her global DSCR is approximately 1.59.

Sophia reinvests her profits and continues to grow her portfolio. Over time, her net operating income increases to $500,000, while her debt service remains at $270,000. Her global DSCR improves to approximately 1.85.

At this stage, Sophia has built a scalable system that allows her to consistently acquire and manage properties. Her strong financial performance and track record position her for further growth.

Now consider the impact of inconsistency. If Sophia had not implemented a system and allowed her properties to perform inconsistently, her DSCR might have dropped below acceptable levels, limiting her ability to acquire additional assets.

This example demonstrates the power of a repeatable system. By maintaining consistency, improving performance, and reinvesting profits, Sophia is able to grow her portfolio systematically.

It also highlights the importance of discipline and strategy. Each decision contributes to the overall success of the system, and maintaining focus on long-term goals is essential.

By applying these principles, you can create a system that allows you to move beyond individual transactions and build a portfolio that generates consistent income and long-term financial freedom.

Chapter 14

Creating Long-Term Wealth, Tax Advantages, and Exit Strategies with SBA Commercial Mortgage Loans

As you reach this advanced stage of your SBA commercial mortgage journey, the focus shifts beyond acquisition and approval into true wealth creation. The most successful borrowers are not just focused on getting loans or buying properties—they are focused on building long-term wealth through strategic ownership, tax efficiency, and well-planned exit strategies. SBA financing is not just a tool for purchasing real estate or businesses; it is a powerful vehicle for creating financial freedom, generational wealth, and long-term stability. In this chapter, you will learn how to maximize the financial benefits of SBA loans through appreciation, cash flow, tax advantages, and strategic exits.

At the core of wealth creation is ownership. When you acquire commercial real estate or a business using SBA financing, you are not just making payments—you are building equity. Each loan payment reduces the principal balance, increasing your ownership stake in the asset. Over time, this creates a powerful compounding effect where your net worth grows as your debt decreases. Unlike renting, where payments provide no long-term benefit, ownership allows you to capture both equity and appreciation.

Appreciation is another key driver of wealth. As property values increase over time, the value of your asset grows, often at a rate that exceeds inflation. This creates additional equity that can be leveraged for future investments. While appreciation is influenced by market conditions, strategic property selection and improvements can enhance value. For example, improving the condition of a property, increasing occupancy, or enhancing revenue streams can lead to higher valuations.

Cash flow is equally important. A well-structured SBA loan should result in positive cash flow, meaning the income generated by the property or business exceeds the expenses and loan payments. This surplus income can be reinvested, used to build reserves, or distributed as profit. Consistent cash flow provides financial stability and supports long-term growth.

One of the most powerful but often misunderstood aspects of SBA financing is the tax advantages associated with ownership. Commercial real estate and business ownership offer several tax benefits that can significantly improve your overall financial position. These include depreciation, interest deductions, and expense write-offs. Depreciation allows you to reduce taxable income by accounting for the gradual wear and tear of a property, even if its market value is increasing. This can result in substantial tax savings.

Interest deductions are another major benefit. The interest portion of your loan payments is typically tax-deductible, reducing your overall tax liability. As interest is often a significant portion of early loan payments, this deduction can provide meaningful financial relief.

Operating expenses related to the property or business are also deductible. This includes costs such as maintenance, utilities, insurance, and management fees. These deductions reduce taxable income and improve net profitability.

Another advanced tax strategy involves cost segregation. This involves breaking down the components of a property to accelerate depreciation on certain elements. By doing this, you can increase your depreciation deductions in the early years of ownership, further reducing taxable income. While this strategy requires professional guidance, it can significantly enhance the financial benefits of ownership.

Understanding how to work with professionals, such as accountants and tax advisors, is critical in maximizing these benefits. Proper planning and documentation ensure that you take full advantage of available deductions while remaining compliant with tax regulations.

Exit strategies are another essential component of long-term wealth building. While acquiring assets is important, knowing how and when to exit is equally critical. There are several exit strategies to consider, each with its own advantages.

One common strategy is holding the asset long-term to maximize cash flow and appreciation. This approach focuses on building wealth gradually over time and creating a stable income stream. It is often the preferred strategy for those seeking financial independence.

Another strategy is refinancing. As property values increase and loan balances decrease, you may have the opportunity to refinance your loan to access equity or secure better terms. This can improve cash flow or provide capital for additional investments.

Selling the asset is another option. If market conditions are favorable, selling can result in significant profits. However, it is important to consider tax implications, such as capital gains taxes, and plan accordingly.

Another advanced strategy is using a 1031 exchange, which allows you to defer capital gains taxes by reinvesting the proceeds from a sale into another property. While SBA loans have specific requirements, understanding how to transition between different types of financing can support this strategy.

Portfolio optimization is another important concept. This involves evaluating your assets and making strategic decisions about which ones to hold, improve, refinance, or sell. The goal is to maximize overall performance and align your portfolio with your long-term objectives.

Risk management is also critical in this phase. Market conditions, economic changes, and operational challenges can impact your investments. Maintaining reserves, diversifying your portfolio, and monitoring performance can help mitigate these risks.

Another key concept is leveraging equity for growth. As your assets appreciate and your equity increases, you can use that equity to acquire additional properties or businesses. This creates a cycle of growth where each asset contributes to the expansion of your portfolio.

Financial independence is achieved when your cash flow from investments covers your living expenses. SBA financing can play a significant role in reaching this goal by enabling you to acquire income-producing assets with favorable terms. Legacy building is another important consideration. Your portfolio can serve as a foundation for future generations, providing both financial security and opportunities. Planning for succession and structuring your assets appropriately ensures that your wealth can be preserved and passed on.

Another important aspect is aligning your strategy with your personal goals. Whether your focus is on income, growth, or legacy, your approach to SBA financing should reflect your priorities. This alignment ensures that your decisions support your long-term vision.

Continuous education and adaptation are also essential. Markets change, regulations evolve, and new opportunities emerge. Staying informed and adapting your strategy allows you to remain competitive and successful.

Ultimately, wealth creation through SBA commercial mortgage loans is about more than numbers—it is about strategy, discipline, and vision. By understanding and applying these principles, you can transform your investments into a powerful engine for financial growth.

This chapter brings together the concepts of ownership, cash flow, tax advantages, and exit strategies into a comprehensive approach to wealth building. By mastering these elements, you can move beyond individual transactions and create a sustainable and growing financial future.

Real-Life Math Example: Building Wealth Through Cash Flow, Equity, and Tax Benefits

Consider an investor named Olivia who purchases a commercial property for $1,000,000 using an SBA loan. She puts down $100,000, resulting in a loan amount of $900,000. The annual debt service is approximately $85,000.

The property generates $140,000 in net operating income, resulting in a DSCR of approximately 1.65. After paying the loan, Olivia has $55,000 in annual cash flow before taxes.

Over the first year, Olivia pays down $20,000 of the loan principal. This increases her equity from $100,000 to $120,000. At the same time, the property appreciates by 5 percent, increasing its value to $1,050,000. Her total equity now becomes $150,000.

Olivia also benefits from depreciation. Assuming she can depreciate $30,000 annually, this reduces her taxable income. Her taxable income is calculated as $55,000 minus $30,000, which equals $25,000. This significantly reduces her tax liability.

In addition, the interest portion of her loan payments, approximately $60,000 in the first year, is also deductible. This further reduces her taxable income, potentially bringing it close to zero. Over five years, Olivia continues to build equity and increase cash flow. Her net operating income grows to $170,000, while her debt service remains at $85,000. Her annual cash flow increases to $85,000.

Her loan balance decreases to approximately $800,000, while the property value increases to $1,200,000. Her equity now stands at $400,000.

At this point, Olivia considers refinancing. By refinancing at a lower interest rate, she reduces her annual debt service to $75,000, increasing her cash flow to $95,000.

Alternatively, she could sell the property. If she sells for $1,200,000 and pays off the remaining loan balance of $800,000, she is left with $400,000 before taxes. Using a 1031 exchange, she could reinvest this amount into a larger property, continuing to grow her portfolio.

This example demonstrates how multiple factors—cash flow, appreciation, loan amortization, and tax benefits—work together to create wealth. Olivia's initial investment of $100,000 grows significantly over time through strategic ownership and management.

If Olivia had not leveraged SBA financing, she might not have been able to acquire the property or achieve the same level of growth. This highlights the power of SBA loans as a tool for wealth creation.

By understanding these principles and applying them strategically, you can build a portfolio that generates income, increases in value, and provides long-term financial security.

Chapter 15

The Complete SBA Commercial Mortgage Blueprint – From First Deal to Financial Independence

At this point in your journey through the SBA Commercial Mortgage Loan Mastery Series, you have developed a comprehensive understanding of how to qualify, structure, secure, and scale SBA commercial mortgage loans. This final chapter brings everything together into a complete, repeatable blueprint—a system you can follow from your very first deal all the way to building a portfolio that supports financial independence and long-term wealth. The purpose of this chapter is not to introduce new concepts, but to integrate everything you have learned into a clear, actionable framework that you can apply immediately and repeatedly.

The SBA blueprint begins with clarity of purpose. Every successful borrower starts with a clear understanding of their goals. Whether your objective is to replace your income, build a real estate portfolio, acquire businesses, or create generational wealth, your strategy must align with that vision. Without clarity, it is easy to pursue deals that do not contribute to your long-term objectives. With clarity, every decision becomes intentional and aligned with your desired outcome.

The first step in the blueprint is building a strong borrower foundation. This includes optimizing your credit, increasing liquidity, organizing your financials, and developing relevant experience. This foundation determines how lenders perceive you and sets the stage for every deal that follows. A strong borrower profile not only increases your chances of approval but also positions you for better terms and greater flexibility.

The second step is identifying the right opportunity. This involves sourcing deals that align with SBA guidelines and your financial goals. The best opportunities are those that combine strong cash flow, reasonable purchase prices, and potential for growth. Evaluating deals systematically allows you to filter out weak opportunities and focus on those that meet your criteria.

The third step is structuring the deal strategically. This includes determining the appropriate loan program, down payment, loan amount, and terms. The goal is to create a structure that maximizes cash flow, meets lender requirements, and minimizes risk. This step requires a deep understanding of how each variable affects DSCR and overall deal strength.

The fourth step is preparing and packaging your loan file. This involves gathering all required documentation, ensuring accuracy and consistency, and presenting your application in a clear and professional manner. A well-prepared loan package builds confidence and accelerates the approval process.

The fifth step is navigating underwriting and conditions. This is where your preparation is tested. Responding to conditions quickly and effectively, maintaining stability, and communicating clearly with your lender are critical to moving your loan toward approval.

The sixth step is closing and funding the deal. This includes satisfying final conditions, executing legal documents, and ensuring that all funds are properly verified and transferred. Attention to detail during this stage ensures a smooth transition from approval to ownership.

The seventh step is post-closing performance. Once the deal is funded, your focus shifts to managing the asset effectively. This includes maintaining strong cash flow, controlling expenses, and ensuring that the property or business performs as expected. Strong performance not only supports the current loan but also positions you for future opportunities.

The eighth step is scaling. As you build equity and improve cash flow, you can leverage your success to acquire additional assets. This involves reinvesting profits, maintaining strong financials, and using your track record to secure additional financing. Scaling transforms individual deals into a portfolio.

The ninth step is optimization. This includes refining your portfolio, improving performance, and making strategic decisions about refinancing, selling, or reinvesting. Optimization ensures that your portfolio continues to grow and align with your goals.

The tenth and final step is achieving financial independence. This occurs when your portfolio generates enough income to cover your living expenses and support your desired lifestyle. At this stage, your focus shifts from growth to preservation and legacy building.

Throughout this blueprint, consistency is key. Each step builds on the previous one, creating a system that can be repeated and refined over time. The more you follow this system, the more efficient and effective you become.

Another important aspect of the blueprint is adaptability. While the framework provides structure, each deal is unique. Being able to adjust your approach based on specific circumstances allows you to navigate challenges and seize opportunities.

Discipline is also essential. Building a portfolio requires patience, persistence, and a commitment to long-term goals. Avoiding impulsive decisions and staying focused on your strategy ensures sustainable growth. Another critical factor is learning from experience. Each deal provides insights that can be used to improve your approach. By continuously refining your system, you increase your chances of success with each transaction.

Building a team is another important component of the blueprint. Working with professionals such as lenders, brokers, accountants, and advisors provides support and expertise that can enhance your results. A strong team allows you to focus on strategy while ensuring that each aspect of the process is handled effectively.

Technology and systems also play a role in scalability. Using tools to manage finances, track performance, and organize documentation can improve efficiency and reduce errors. As your portfolio grows, these systems become increasingly important.

Risk management is integrated throughout the blueprint. This includes maintaining reserves, diversifying your portfolio, and ensuring that each deal has a margin of safety. Managing risk effectively allows you to navigate challenges without jeopardizing your progress.

Another important concept is compounding. As you reinvest profits and leverage your assets, your portfolio grows at an accelerating rate. This compounding effect is one of the most powerful aspects of SBA financing. Legacy building is the final layer of the blueprint. Beyond financial success, your portfolio can provide opportunities and security for future generations. Structuring your assets and planning for succession ensures that your wealth can be preserved and passed on.

Ultimately, the SBA blueprint is about transformation. It is about moving from a single transaction to a system that creates consistent results. It is about turning knowledge into action and action into long-term success.

This chapter represents the culmination of everything you have learned. By following this blueprint, you can move from your first SBA loan to building a portfolio that supports financial independence and beyond.

Real-Life Math Example: Applying the SBA Blueprint from First Deal to Financial Independence

Consider an investor named Ethan who begins with a single SBA loan to purchase a property for $800,000. He puts down $80,000, resulting in a loan amount of $720,000. The annual debt service is approximately $65,000. The property generates a net operating income of $110,000, resulting in a DSCR of approximately 1.69.

In the first year, Ethan focuses on improving performance. He increases net operating income to $120,000, raising his DSCR to approximately 1.85. He also pays down $15,000 of the loan principal, increasing his equity.

Using his improved financial position, Ethan acquires a second property for $1,000,000 with a down payment of $100,000 and a loan amount of $900,000. The annual debt service is approximately $85,000, and the property generates a net operating income of $130,000, resulting in a DSCR of 1.53.

Ethan's combined portfolio now generates $250,000 in net operating income with total debt service of $150,000. His global DSCR is approximately 1.67.

Over the next two years, Ethan continues to improve performance and acquire additional properties. He adds a third property generating $150,000 in net operating income with debt service of $100,000, and a fourth property generating $170,000 with debt service of $115,000.

His total portfolio now generates $570,000 in net operating income with total debt service of $365,000. His global DSCR is approximately 1.56.

Ethan's annual cash flow after debt service is $205,000. He reinvests a portion of this income while using the rest to support his lifestyle. As his portfolio grows, Ethan reaches a point where his cash flow exceeds his living expenses of $150,000 per year. At this stage, he achieves financial independence. Ethan continues to optimize his portfolio by refinancing properties, reducing interest rates, and increasing cash flow. His net operating income grows to $650,000 while debt service remains at $365,000, increasing his annual cash flow to $285,000.

Now consider the long-term impact. Ethan's initial investment of $80,000 has grown into a portfolio generating hundreds of thousands of dollars in annual income. His equity has increased significantly through loan amortization and property appreciation.

If Ethan had not followed a structured approach, he might have struggled to scale or maintain performance. By applying the SBA blueprint, he was able to build a sustainable and growing portfolio.

This example demonstrates the power of a systematic approach to SBA financing. By following each step of the blueprint, Ethan transforms a single deal into a portfolio that supports financial independence.

It also highlights the importance of consistency, discipline, and strategic thinking. Each decision contributes to the overall success of the system. By applying these principles, you can create your own blueprint for success and achieve your financial goals through SBA commercial mortgage loans.

Closing Thoughts

From Knowledge to Execution—Your Path Forward

As you reach the end of this book, it is important to recognize that what you now possess is far more than information. You now have a complete framework for understanding, navigating, and mastering SBA commercial mortgage financing. You have seen how deals are structured, how lenders think, how approvals are achieved, and how portfolios are built over time. But the true value of this knowledge lies not in what you have read—it lies in what you choose to do next. Execution is the bridge between knowledge and results, and your ability to take action will determine the outcome of everything you have learned.

The SBA loan process, when viewed from the outside, can appear complex, slow, and even intimidating. But as you have seen throughout this series, it is actually a system—a predictable, structured process that rewards preparation, clarity, and strategy. Once you understand how each component works and how they connect, the process becomes far more manageable. You begin to see patterns. You begin to anticipate outcomes. And most importantly, you begin to take control. One of the most powerful shifts you can make moving forward is adopting the mindset of a strategic borrower rather than a reactive applicant. Reactive borrowers wait for lenders to tell them what is needed, respond to requests as they arise, and hope for approval. Strategic borrowers, on the other hand, prepare in advance, structure deals intentionally, and present their applications in a way that aligns with lender expectations from the very beginning. This shift in mindset alone can dramatically increase your success rate.

It is also important to understand that progress in this space is cumulative. Your first deal may require more effort, more learning, and more adjustments. But each deal that follows becomes easier as your experience grows. Your understanding deepens. Your systems improve. Your relationships strengthen. Over time, what once felt complex becomes routine. What once required significant effort becomes efficient. This is the power of repetition and refinement.

Another key takeaway is that perfection is not required—progress is. Many potential borrowers delay taking action because they feel their profile is not strong enough or their deal is not perfect. While preparation is important, waiting for perfection can lead to missed opportunities. The reality is that most successful borrowers improve their profiles and refine their strategies through action, not before it. Each step forward provides valuable feedback that allows you to improve. You have also seen that challenges are part of the process. Whether it is a condition during underwriting, a delay in documentation, or even a loan denial, these challenges are not barriers—they are opportunities to learn and improve. The most successful borrowers are those who approach challenges with a problem-solving mindset. They analyze what went wrong, make the necessary adjustments, and move forward with greater clarity.

Financial discipline is another cornerstone of long-term success. Building a portfolio through SBA financing requires careful management of cash flow, reserves, and expenses. Each decision you make should strengthen your financial position rather than weaken it. This discipline not only supports your current investments but also positions you for future opportunities.

Another important concept is patience. While the SBA process can take time, the long-term benefits far outweigh the initial investment of effort. Building a portfolio is not a quick process—it is a journey that unfolds over years. But with each step, you move closer to financial stability, independence, and freedom. Patience allows you to make thoughtful decisions and avoid unnecessary risks.

It is also essential to maintain a long-term perspective. The goal is not just to complete a single transaction but to create a system that can be repeated and scaled. Each deal should contribute to your overall strategy and move you closer to your goals. By thinking long-term, you can make decisions that support sustainable growth rather than short-term gains.

Another powerful takeaway is the importance of relationships. Lenders, brokers, advisors, and partners all play a role in your success. Building strong, professional relationships creates opportunities, provides support, and enhances your credibility. These relationships can become one of your most valuable assets as you continue to grow.

As you move forward, it is important to stay adaptable. Markets change, interest rates fluctuate, and new opportunities emerge. Being able to adjust your strategy while maintaining your core principles allows you to navigate these changes effectively. Adaptability ensures that you remain resilient and responsive in a dynamic environment.

Continuous learning is also critical. While this book provides a comprehensive foundation, the world of commercial finance is always evolving. Staying informed, seeking new knowledge, and refining your approach will keep you ahead and allow you to capitalize on emerging opportunities.

Another key concept is confidence. Confidence comes from preparation, understanding, and experience. As you apply what you have learned and begin to see results, your confidence will grow. This confidence will influence how you approach deals, interact with lenders, and make decisions. It becomes a powerful driver of success.

It is also important to recognize the broader impact of what you are building. Beyond financial returns, you are creating opportunities—for yourself, your family, and potentially others. You are building assets that generate income, support businesses, and contribute to economic activity. This perspective adds meaning and purpose to your efforts.

Legacy is another important consideration. The assets and systems you build can extend beyond your lifetime, providing stability and opportunities for future generations. Thinking about how your portfolio can be structured and managed over time ensures that your efforts have a lasting impact.

As you reflect on everything you have learned, remember that the journey does not end here. This is not a conclusion—it is a beginning. You now have the knowledge, the framework, and the tools to move forward with clarity and purpose. The next step is to take action.

Start by evaluating your current position. Review your financials, assess your goals, and identify your next opportunity. Use the principles you have learned to structure your deal, prepare your application, and approach lenders with confidence. Take the first step, knowing that each step after will become easier.

Stay consistent in your approach. Follow the system. Refine your process. Learn from each experience. Over time, you will build momentum, and that momentum will carry you forward.

Most importantly, believe in your ability to succeed. The process you have learned is not reserved for a select few—it is accessible to anyone who is willing to understand it and apply it. You now have that understanding.

Your future in SBA commercial mortgage financing is not determined by chance—it is shaped by your actions. The knowledge is in your hands. The opportunity is in front of you. The path is clear.

Now it is time to walk it.

How to Get a Personalized SBA Commercial Mortgage Review

If you found this book helpful, you may want to see how these strategies apply to your specific financial situation.

SBA commercial mortgage financing is highly customized—your business income, financial statements, credit profile, property type, industry, and long-term goals all play a role in determining what you qualify for and how your loan should be structured.

Every borrower's situation is different. Your revenue trends, business model, tax returns, debt obligations, ownership structure, and the type of commercial property you are purchasing, refinancing, or building all impact your options. The strategies and examples in this book are designed to teach you how SBA commercial mortgage loans work—but your actual loan approval, terms, and structure can only be determined by analyzing your real financial profile.

If you would like a no-obligation SBA Commercial Mortgage review, you can request one here:

Email: info@FinibiMortgage.com

A licensed mortgage broker will review your business financials, income structure, credit profile, and goals, and explain what SBA financing options may be available to you—including:

• SBA 7(a) commercial mortgage loans• SBA 504 fixed-rate commercial real estate financing• Owner-occupied property qualification strategies• Business acquisition with real estate financing• Commercial refinance and cash-out strategies• Construction and expansion loan structuring• Advanced SBA deal structuring to maximize approval

No cost. No pressure. No obligation.

Sincerely,

Joseph G. Correa

Finibi Mortgage Inc.

Licensed Mortgage Broker

About the Author

Joseph G. Correa is a licensed mortgage broker and the founder of Finibi Mortgage, a Florida-based brokerage specializing in SBA commercial mortgage loans, non-QM lending, and strategic real estate financing solutions for business owners, entrepreneurs, and investors.

With more than two decades of experience in mortgage lending, underwriting, and deal structuring, Joseph has helped thousands of clients secure financing for commercial real estate, business acquisitions, and complex transactions using both traditional and alternative lending strategies.

Unlike traditional loan officers who focus only on basic qualification, Joseph's approach emphasizes **cash flow analysis, deal structuring, and strategic financing**. He believes that business owners should not be limited by rigid lending formulas, but instead empowered by understanding how to structure deals that align with lender guidelines and maximize approval potential.

Joseph is widely recognized for his expertise in:

• SBA 7(a) and SBA 504 commercial mortgage loans• Owner-occupied commercial real estate financing• Business acquisition with real estate structuring• Commercial refinance and cash flow optimization• Construction and expansion financing• Advanced loan structuring and approval strategy

Through his education platform, Finibi Academy, Joseph has trained tens of thousands of students worldwide in mortgage strategy, real estate investing, credit optimization, and financial independence.

He created the *SBA Commercial Mortgage Loan Mastery Series* to provide a clear, step-by-step roadmap for borrowers and professionals who want to understand, qualify for, and scale commercial real estate using SBA financing.

His mission is simple:

To help business owners use strategic financing to acquire assets, build cash flow, and create long-term wealth.

When he is not structuring loans or writing, Joseph works with clients across the United States to design customized SBA financing strategies aligned with their business goals and growth plans.

The SBA Commercial Mortgage Loan Mastery Series Roadmap

The Complete Guide to Using SBA Financing to Build Commercial Real Estate and Business Wealth

The purpose of *The SBA Commercial Mortgage Loan Mastery Series* is to give business owners, investors, and mortgage professionals the exact strategies used by lenders and underwriters—translated into simple, practical steps you can apply in real life.

This series takes you from beginner to advanced mastery of how to qualify, structure, and scale commercial real estate and business financing using SBA mortgage loans.

Each book builds on the last. You are not just learning how to get approved—you are learning how to control your approvals and scale your opportunities.

Book 1 — SBA Commercial Mortgage Loan Fundamentals Understand how SBA mortgage programs work, including 7(a) and 504 loans, and how to qualify.

Book 2 — Getting Approved for an SBA Commercial Mortgage Loan Learn step-by-step strategies to meet lender requirements and secure funding.

Book 3 — Owner-Occupied Property Financing with SBA Loans Learn how to buy or refinance your business property using SBA financing.

Book 4 — Buying a Business and Real Estate with SBA Financing Acquire a business and its property in one structured transaction.

Book 5 — SBA 7(a) Mortgage Loan Strategies Master flexible loan structures for business and real estate funding.

Book 6 — SBA 504 Mortgage Loans for Commercial Real Estate Use long-term fixed-rate financing for large property acquisitions.

Book 7 — Refinancing Commercial Debt with SBA Loans Lower payments, improve cash flow, and restructure existing debt.

Book 8 — SBA Loans for Construction and Expansion Build, renovate, and scale commercial properties with structured financing.

Book 9 — SBA Loan Requirements, Rates, and Structures Understand how to compare options and choose the best loan.

Book 10 — Advanced SBA Commercial Mortgage Structuring Engineer approvals and maximize leverage using expert strategies.

This series is designed to move you from:

Understanding → Execution → Scaling → Mastery

By the end, you will not just know how to qualify—you will know how to structure, analyze, and scale deals like a professional.

Educational & Financial Disclaimer

The *SBA Commercial Mortgage Loan Mastery Series* is intended for educational and informational purposes only.

This content is designed to help readers understand SBA commercial mortgage lending, real estate financing strategies, and business acquisition concepts. It is not financial, legal, tax, or investment advice.

Joseph G. Correa and Live Stronger Faster are not acting as your personal financial advisor, attorney, accountant, or mortgage professional through this publication.

SBA loan programs, underwriting guidelines, interest rates, and lender requirements may change at any time and vary by lender.

All examples in this series are for illustration purposes only and do not guarantee approval or results.

Always consult with licensed professionals before making financial decisions.

Risk Disclosure

SBA commercial mortgage lending and real estate investing involve risk.

Business performance, income stability, interest rate changes, market conditions, and lender guidelines can all impact loan approval and financial outcomes.

Borrowing against real estate or using leverage increases both potential returns and risk.

Failure to repay a loan may result in foreclosure and loss of property.

Cash flow, rental income, appreciation, and business performance are not guaranteed.

All strategies presented in this series are educational and must be evaluated based on your individual financial situation.

You are solely responsible for your financial decisions.

www.ingramcontent.com/pod-product-compliance
Ingram Content Group UK Ltd.
Pitfield, Milton Keynes, MK11 3LW, UK
UKHW020159290926
15471UKWH00005B/960